MIND ON EDGE

CLINGING TO FAITH WHEN MENTAL HEALTH FADES

Tom Hogsed

Mind On Edge: Clinging To Faith When Mental Health Fades
Copyright © 2019 Tom Hogsed
Print ISBN: 9781089004639

All rights reserved. No part of this publication may be reproduced, stored in a retrieval system, or transmitted in any form or by any means - electronic, mechanical, photocopy, recording, or any other - except for brief quotations in printed reviews, without prior permission of the author.

SCRIPTURE USAGE

Scripture quotations marked ESV are taken from The ESV® Bible (The Holy Bible, English Standard Version®), copyright © 2001 by Crossway, a publishing ministry of Good News Publishers. Used by permission. All rights reserved.

Scripture quotations marked NKJV are taken from the New King James Version®. Copyright © 1982 by Thomas Nelson. Used by permission. All rights reserved.

Scripture quotations marked NLT are taken from the Holy Bible, New Living Translation, copyright ©1996, 2004, 2015 by Tyndale House Foundation. Used by permission of Tyndale House Publishers, Inc., Carol Stream, Illinois 60188. All rights reserved.

BOOK COVER

Photo: Mental Health by Wildpixel from Getty Images Pro (via canva.com)

Design: Designed using canva.com

DEDICATION

There are so many people to whom I could dedicate this book, but I want to express a huge appreciation to anyone who cares deeply about the mental well-being of themselves or others. It takes courage to pick up a book labeled mental health. Getting a book about mental health is not an admission of defeat but determination. It's an acknowledgment of weakness, but not worthlessness.

I would also like to recognize the people who have opened up to me about your struggles with mental health. I have always felt as if my counsel was genuine, but never enough. Even though I have spent countless hours with some of you and recommended additional resources, I always wanted to give you more because you deserve it.

I also dedicate these words to people who have felt overlooked and unnoticed by the church. When you said, "I'm depressed or anxious" they told you that if you pray and read your Bible more, the feelings will go away. I'm not questioning the church's intention, but their involvement. God expects His people to *walk with*, not *walk away* from those who are struggling with being mentally healthy.

It may sound cliché, but I want to dedicate these words to the Lord. This book is about making His name great. It's about helping people see God through their adversity and holding on to the hope we have in redemption. All of us await the day when our minds will not be on edge, but free from the cares and worries of this life.

ACKNOWLEDGEMENTS

My wife and kids deserve to be recognized. None of them asked to live in a pastor's home, but they have done it with grace. I'm sure they feel the pressure of people always watching, which is a natural part of being in ministry. You have extended mercy to me as I speak from Scripture to our church family each week on areas in which I am still struggling. Never once have you told me I'm unqualified to talk about something just because I didn't have it all together.

My parents and brothers are also a big part of my life. Even though distance separates us, I believe those first 18 years of my life gave me a picture of how imperfect people can live and love, even in the messiness of life. Todd, I have always admired your ability to light up a room. Tim, I have always admired your ability to think deeply on many levels yet remain open to differing opinions. Mom and Dad, the power of both of you spending time with us and being proud of us has meant the world. I would not change a thing, except the time Mom wouldn't let me wear Birkenstocks without socks to Sunday night church. Jesus wore sandals.

My church family, The Summit, has been a big part of my life for more than a decade. Even though my title is Lead Pastor, I feel that you lead me. When we launched the Summit Church, I was inexperienced and scared to admit that I did not always know what I was doing or how to do it. You have been gracious in your love and supportive of God's calling in my life. I'm a better person because of you. While I was writing this book, I was thinking of the people in our church family who wrestle with mental health. I don't talk about your stories in these pages, but your stories are always on my mind. I hope you know that you are not alone.

CONTENTS

Introduction: My Story and Hope 9

Chapter 1: Tracing the Origins of Mental Health 21

Chapter 2: Finding God Amid Mental Illness 35

Chapter 3: Peace - The Guarding of Your Heart and Mind 49

Chapter 4: Patience - The Hope of Your Heart and Mind 67

Chapter 5: Love - The Strength of Your Heart and Mind 79

Chapter 6: Confession - The Renewal of Your Heart and Mind 95

Chapter 7: Comfort - The Testimony of Your Heart and Mind 111

Chapter 8: What's My Next Step? 123

Resources for Mental Health 135

INTRODUCTION: MY STORY AND HOPE

> "If the Lord had not been my help, my soul would soon have lived in the land of silence. When I thought, 'My foot slips,' your steadfast love, O Lord, held me up. When the cares of my heart are many, your consolations cheer my soul. (Psalm 94:17-19, ESV)

Jared pulled into his garage, turned off the car, and pressed the button to shut the door behind him. He was glad to finally be home, so he just sat in the dark garage with his hands still gripping the steering wheel. His mind was racing. He never recalled his parents going through any major struggles with their feelings. They had talked about *mid-life* crisis, but not *mental* health. Jared remembered hearing his Mom and Dad sarcastically talk about mid-life in terms of buying a sports car, switching jobs or locations, and losing athletic ability, but he could not recollect anyone talking about what a person is supposed to do when they feel low. Most conversations about "seasons of life" focused on *actions*, not *feelings*. Discussions usually centered on what people *do*, not how they *feel*. To Jared, *managing actions* seemed a lot easier than *managing feelings* at this stage in his life. He was 39 years old and empty. Those closest to him said he was mildly depressed or just anxious about getting older. They told him it would pass. That was two years ago, and the feelings had only gotten stronger. Over the last couple years, he tried to fix the way he felt and although he made progress, it had been short-lived.

As he reflected on the current significance of his life, he did not have many complaints. There were some things he would change, but he was unsure if changing actions would change the way he felt. If only he could align his *attitude* with his *accomplishments*. His past successes were not enough to sustain him through his present feelings.

He was indifferent rather than interested.
Restless rather than rested.
Envious rather than encouraging.
Drifting rather than directed.

Jared felt empty. He was just exhausted from all the mental games. He did not know when these feelings began and rightfully assumed that they had been occurring *over time* not *overnight*. Jared knew that something had to change. He resisted putting a label on the way he was feeling, but knew he was struggling with a mind that was on edge. Depression? Anxiety? Maybe some other label?

Liz could not put her phone down. She had just posted on Facebook about a recent job promotion she had received and was hoping the "likes" would start pouring in. Liz already knew that she spent a lot of time on social media, but this particular day she needed the validation of her friends, family, and acquaintances. It had been a rough 6 months for Liz. Most people did not know she was in the hospital for a couple days because she was struggling through a low point in her life. She was proud that she had taken the step to get help, but the recovery from her depression and anxiety was not moving as quickly as she hoped. This job promotion was a mental boost for her. She needed something to swing her way, and this was it. Now she wanted everyone else to celebrate with her.

Throughout the day she kept checking her phone. She received several "likes" on her post and a couple people even wrote congratulatory words, but toward the end of the day Liz was frustrated by the people who hadn't acknowledged her post. She scrolled through her list of friends (if that's what she could call them) to see who had not recognized her announcement. Liz spent a lot of time "liking" and commenting on others' posts when they revealed moments worthy of applauding, but why would they not show her the same kindness? She googled, "How to delete Facebook account" because she could not take the perceived rejection any longer. Besides, every time she scrolled through her news feed, she closed the app feeling discouraged. Her life was boring and worthless compared to everyone else. The validation Liz was seeking on social media never lived up to her expectations. She was done with social media. She deactivated her account and went to bed angry at those who couldn't take a minute of their time to make her feel good about herself.

Life is filled with struggles – ones we can't control and a few that we can. Some people encounter adversity early on, while difficulties test others after decades of journeying through a relatively problem-free life. There is no simple formula for facing the battles that take place in the mind. It is possible that the largest and longest battles in life will remain invisible to those on the outside.

Much like Jared and Liz's stories, we have *expectations* about how life should be, but are discouraged when life takes an unexpected or unwanted turn. Many of us are not prepared for the mental battles that every human being encounters. How do we cling to faith when our mental health is fading? Allow God to change our *attitude*, even when the *circumstance* does not change.

This book is not a "**You** can do this" message. The words that follow are a "**God** can do this" message. The following words are not necessarily about God taking away mental health struggles, but about us learning to embrace God's sustaining power. If we will allow God's voice to be the loudest, we will be shaped by what He says about us rather than being shaped by what we say to ourselves.

MY STORY

All of us had piled into the car and were making our way from Ohio to visit family in North Carolina. After crossing the state line, I began to feel an overwhelming sense of panic. This was not a typical experience for me, so I pulled into the first rest area I could find and spent the next several minutes trying to calm myself down. I paced back and forth while my mind raced with uncontrollable thoughts. Every breath was a struggle. My wife got out of the car and wanted to know what was going on, but I didn't know how to explain what I was experiencing. I told her, "I feel like I'm dying."

I would later discover I was having a panic attack and it wouldn't be the last episode. A panic attack is a sudden and overwhelming sense of anxiety that seems to hold you captive for a brief time. I couldn't identify the reason for the panic attack, which was frustrating because knowing the cause of a problem usually makes it easier to find a solution. It is not in my nature to await a resolution. I wanted to fix it right away.

These panic attacks began pouncing at the most awkward times. At this point in my life, I had been a pastor for 17 years and regularly spoke to hundreds of people and occasionally to thousands. I had repeatedly taught people at camps and retreats in unfamiliar places. Since I also enjoy traveling internationally, I have spoken at churches in other countries through translators. The panic was not an issue of not knowing *how* to do something, but *what* would happen when I did it.

Delivering regular sermons is a part of my spiritual gifting and something that has always brought fulfillment to my life. But now I suddenly paced back and forth while attempting to control a racing mind before going on stage to deliver a sermon. This wasn't normal. I wasn't myself. After some conversations with my family doctor, he recommended some action steps to help me function normally once again. Getting caught off-guard was not an option. I had people who "depended" on me. Panic was not something that would help me be "strong" for others.

Ups and downs characterized the next few months, but that year ended with me finding it difficult to get out of bed each day. Discouragement and depression set in (things I had only spoken about in sermons) and now I was living them out. I don't know what happened or even when the feelings began, but everything seemed like it was crashing down on me. There were several days I just wanted to die. I believed life was not worth it anymore. My wife encouraged me to get help, so I found myself back in the doctor's office attempting to explain my feelings of despair.

When my doctor asked me how everything was going, I told him I had the normal job and family stresses but did not know why I felt so discouraged. It was difficult to uncover a specific cause that would warrant these types of feelings. My doctor told me I needed to see a counselor. I didn't want to. I had spent my whole life counseling people, and I arrogantly believed that a counselor could not tell me anything I did not already know.

I was wrong. I underestimated the power of someone listening. There are a couple people in my life who listen, but this was different. The counselor didn't have any preconceived feelings or beliefs about me. I could just talk about my life. There was no big moment of discovery, but it gave me an outlet to talk. Because I am a pastor most of what I hear, think, and see stays inside me. This was a rare opportunity to verbalize what I often internalized. I wish I could tell you that seeing a counselor was the magic formula. It wasn't. The counselor felt I needed a bit of help with medication.

Since I had spent most of my life thinking people with mental health struggles should just "suck it up and move on," I found myself in a dilemma. Should I rely on medication to get me through this low point in life? I ended up filling that prescription, and it became a part of my life. I am not recommending medication for every situation. This is only *my* story and *my* experience. I knew how hopeless I felt and a long-term bout with depression would not end well for me. The motivation to pray and read God's Word were lacking. Thoughts of worthlessness dominated my heart and mind. I needed something to help me trend in the right direction. My humble opinion is that medication is only one part of the solution for those who explore that option. You cannot take medication but abandon the fight through mental health struggles. I still have my bad days where I drop low quickly; however, those feelings rarely hang around for weeks and months. There is a greater awareness in my life for when I need some extra help to feel like myself again.

MY HOPE
Now that you have heard a small part of my story, I hope you will allow me to share some of my personal thoughts about mental health. I hope to provide you with a foundation for thinking about this subject. Your struggle may be longer, deeper, and more complicated than mine. Our stories may originate from different places or circumstances. That's okay. What's important in this ongoing dialogue is that you and I embrace a couple steps to help find our way back to being mentally

healthy. Personally, I don't know if a person ever moves beyond mental health battles, but I believe God will use them to keep us dependent on Him.

You may feel weak and worn out.

You may feel as if you cannot take one more step or take a deep breath.

But you can.

Weakness is where God does His best work.

Jesus said, "My power works best in weakness" (2 Corinthians 12:9, NLT).

The words you are about to read in this book are not a "one size fits all." In the pages that follow, we will launch a conversation about being mentally healthy. You may think, "This doesn't fit me exactly." I fully realize that everybody's circumstances are unique, but I want to challenge you to adjust the *size* accordingly. The central thoughts and principles of this book should be equally relevant to everyone, but the application may need a change.

MY CAUTION

I also recognize that some mental health struggles are more severe than others. My heart is to help people battle their thoughts, emotions, and interactions with others; however, this book may only be the beginning of your journey to being mentally healthy, not the end. Finding yourself in a VERY dark place mentally, emotionally, physically, and spiritually is a sign that you may need more immediate help. It's okay to seek professional help. There is no shame in admitting your need for God and others to come alongside you. I would love to promise you that all your problems will go away by reading this book. They won't. But through reading these words, I hope you can gain more clarity on what is happening in your mind and seek further help when necessary.

Please view this book as you would the front door to your home. When you twist the handle and walk inside, the door is only the entrance to a residence filled with many rooms (living room, kitchen, closet, guest bedroom, entertainment room, basement, kid's bedroom). Each of these rooms holds *issues*, and together we will open each door. The tour of these rooms may be painful, but the approach I am taking in the following chapters is to challenge you to stop ignoring what you may already know to be true - you struggle with the thoughts that spin around in your mind and the actions that attach themselves to them. Your mind stays on edge. It rarely settles. It is often in overdrive. You are uncertain where your thoughts will take you.

You may not have a medical diagnosis of a mental health disorder, but EVERYONE knows what it feels like to face discouragement and walk through deep valleys. Even if your thought patterns do not have a label, my prayer is for you to filter your beliefs through the lens of Scripture as we get to know the One who created us.

Maybe you are reading this book to come alongside someone you love who is struggling with their mental health. Blessings to you for caring enough about others to step into their world and help lift them out of a place of hopelessness. The planet needs more people like you - someone who will not watch silently as a friend or family member suffers alone. All of us need to adopt the philosophy of *inviting* rather than *ignoring*. God created us for relationships, and it is wise to have people who breathe life into a withering soul. I hope to be a part of that journey for you, whether these words are for you or for you to help someone else.

MY ASSUMPTION

As we will discover in the first chapter, there is a 50/50 chance that you will experience a diagnosable mental health disorder in your lifetime. So, there are two ways an individual could read this book: **proactively** or **reactively**. My assumption is that most of you are reading *reactively*. This means that your mental health is already suffering, so you reacted by seeking help through research and reading. Having this book in hand is a testimony to this. There is nothing wrong with reading reactively. I commend you for taking steps to get your mental health back!

The second way to read this book is *proactively*. Mental health challenges can strike at any moment, so you are reading before the issue manifests. This means you may not be fighting it at this moment but are preparing for what may be ahead. Just because it's not happening now does not safeguard you from it ever happening. Mental health often changes when seasons of life change or there has been a major transition in your routine. If you are reading proactively, I also commend you for looking ahead.

Whether you are reading proactively or reactively, thank you. I have spent many years listening to the struggles of others and counseling them through their pain. I have spent the last several years living through it. Sometimes I wonder, "Why me?" Other times I wonder, "Why *not* me?" My battles, although minor compared to some, have given me a heart to encourage, challenge, and fight together. I have discovered that I am not meant to suffer alone.

> "Two people are better off than one, for they can help each other succeed. If one person falls, the other can reach out and help. But someone who falls alone is in real trouble. Likewise, two people lying close together can keep each other warm. But how can one be warm

alone? A person standing alone can be attacked and defeated, but two can stand back-to-back and conquer. Three are even better, for a triple-braided cord is not easily broken." (Ecclesiastes 4:9-12, NLT)

MY ADVICE

Please read <u>all</u> the chapters in this book. When we discuss the **FIVE ATTITUDES TO BEING MENTALLY HEALTHY** (Chapters 3-7), many of the steps relate to each other and provide a well-rounded thought process about mental health.

Here is a preview of the attitudes to being mentally healthy.
1) Peace: The Balance of Your Heart and Mind
2) Patience: The Hope of Your Heart and Mind
3) Love: The Strength of Your Heart and Mind
4) Confession: The Renewal of Your Heart and Mind
5) Comfort: The Testimony of Your Heart and Mind

As you read this book, please consider making two declarations.

Declaration #1: If I am mentally unhealthy, I will not be ashamed to seek help from God, professionals, and those who love me. I will not give up the fight with my thoughts.

Declaration #2: If I know someone who is struggling with mental health, I will be quick to listen and offer help. I will not remain silent, exclude, or judge.

These declarations must be made so we can begin helping ourselves and others find the path back to being mentally healthy.

THINK ABOUT IT

At the end of each chapter, there will be a couple of questions or thoughts to help you process the chapter. It will be easy to skip this section, but I am challenging you to look your mental health right in the face AND determine action steps to put you back on a path to being mentally healthy. Avoidance resolves nothing; in fact, it may make matters worse. So, let's start right now.

Why are you reading this book?

When you finish reading this book, what do you hope will happen?

Are you willing to see a professional counselor? Why or why not?

If you are struggling with your mental health, who is the most trusted person you will tell?

Is there someone who would enjoy reading this book with you? If so, reach out to them right now so both of you can verbalize what you have probably been internalizing.

CHAPTER 1: TRACING THE ORIGINS OF MENTAL HEALTH

> "When Adam sinned, sin entered the world. Adam's sin brought death, so death spread to everyone, for everyone sinned." (Romans 5:12, NLT)

Everyone has mental health, whether they are mentally healthy or unhealthy. It is similar to how we think about physical health. Every living person has physical health. Some people are physically healthy, and others are unhealthy. While there is some stigma with being physically unhealthy, there is a sense of shame attached to mental health. Why? Mental health affects us emotionally (how we feel), mentally (how we think), and socially (how we interact with others). Any instability in our mental health determines how we handle stress and make decisions. In addition, our thought-patterns, moods, and behaviors can be affected.[i] Being mentally unhealthy carries a stigma because those who do not understand it may have a low tolerance for someone who is battling a mind on edge. Rather than explaining feelings, fears, and past abuse, it is easier to keep it inside. Few people raise their hand to talk about how they feel alone, anxious, and depressed.

How common are mental health struggles? Some statistics tell us that one in five people experience a diagnosable mental health disorder each year. Research further reveals that nearly 50% of people will experience a mental health disorder in their lifetime. [ii]

This means that if you are not struggling through a mental health battle, someone near you is.

The world is beginning the conversation about mental health, and the church can no longer stay silent. In the past, the church has been guilty of attaching a stigma to mental health disorders. For example, when someone is struggling through a physical sickness, no one hesitates to request prayer. If someone has a heart attack, what do we do? We pray on behalf of that individual. When an individual is harmed in an accident or diagnosed with cancer, we beg God to intervene. Now, consider the last time you heard someone publicly ask prayer for themselves concerning an eating disorder, suicidal thoughts, or depression?

Those who are struggling mentally often struggle alone.

If mental health disorders are as common as we believe them to be, followers of Jesus cannot ignore this issue any longer. When one out of every five people inside and outside of our churches are struggling with being mentally unhealthy then silence, exclusion, and judgment are not appropriate responses.

The mental health crisis just came to light for me a couple years ago. Unfortunately, when I began my vocation as a leader in the church over 20 years ago, I contemplated whether mental health struggles were real. "Why can't he just get over it?", I thought. "Why can't she just move past this?" I even encouraged people to "have more faith" or "snap out of it" as if being mentally unhealthy is a switch to turn off and on. After years of reading examples of people in the Bible and God allowing certain experiences in my life, I am gaining a different perspective, a perspective that leaves me with some regrets about the lack of empathy I held from people who expected and needed it.

What types of mental health struggles are people facing and how are they defined? Although that list could extend several pages, the following will serve as tangible examples. It is not an exhaustive list but highlights more common ones.

- *Anxiety Disorders* - actions, reactions, or thought patterns that are not appropriate for a circumstance
- *Drug and Alcohol Addictions* - the overuse of a legal or illegal substance to eliminate feelings of anxiety, depression, or trauma
- *Eating Disorders* - strong emotions, attitudes, and actions involving a person's view of food and their weight
- *Mood Disorders* - ongoing feelings of discouragement; short periods of time feeling extremely happy; frequent swings between discouragement and happiness (some examples include depression, bipolar disorder, or seasonal affective disorder)
- *Obsessive-Compulsive Disorder (OCD)* - persistent thoughts and/or phobias that cause an individual to perform rituals or routines
- *Personality Disorders* – exaggerated personality characteristics which cause stress to the individual and may present difficulty in a person's interactions at their school, workplace, or social relationships
- *Post-Traumatic Stress Disorder (PTSD)* – may arise after a traumatic or disturbing event (abuse, death, war, or a natural disaster) and results in ongoing memories or thoughts of that event
- *Psychotic Disorders* - distorted reality in a person's attentiveness and reasoning[iii]

Some of you may read this list and question the validity of these disorders. Let's be honest, though. These feelings, actions, and reactions have ALWAYS existed (following sin), but now we have labels for them. It is possible that these human-prescribed labels have caused us to believe that they are a modern invention. Maybe you frequently approach mental health with skepticism and have rendered a negative judgment on those who seem to struggle. You do not believe these disorders exist. You live by a **principle of experience**.

What is the **principle of experience**? It is a concept that only embraces something when my experience has led me to believe it to be true.

It is a dangerous principle to live by because the foundation of our belief system then rests in subjective experiences. "If I believe it to be true, it's true; and, if I believe it to be false, it's not true." This principle upholds a person's opinion and experience as the only truth. Let's not "play counselor" based on our own experiences. Have enough wisdom to realize that everyone's experience is not like your own. Comprising a list of mental disorders may be easy, but discovering *why* they exist is a little more intricate. Most health professionals believe there are a couple of factors that affect mental health.[iv]

- Biological Factors (genetics, brain chemistry, disease, injury)
- Life Experiences (trauma or abuse)
- Family History (observational)

BIOLOGICAL FACTORS

I am not a doctor. I will not pretend to understand the complexities of the body and brain. There are professionals more qualified and experienced than me in this area. Abnormalities in genes, family history, brain injuries, and disease can negatively affect mental health. I do not mean this book to dissect biological factors and provide a solution. If you (or someone you love) may be mentally unhealthy because of biological factors, I recommend seeking professional help. This is an important step for someone who experiences mentally unhealthy patterns because they not only affect the individual but also the people they love. Believing that biological factors will improve over time may delay the road to healing.

LIFE EXPERIENCES

My heart bleeds for anyone who has ever experienced trauma or abuse. It is regrettable that we live in a world where abuse is common in homes, schools, marriages, social gatherings, places of employment, and even churches. Environments once deemed *safe* are littered with the casualties of abuse. There is a two-fold way to heal from mental health related to abuse.

First, **tell someone**. Not just anyone, but someone who you trust. An honest conversation with a trustworthy individual can begin moving a person in the right direction. This step may necessitate professional and/or long-term counseling for the victim.

The second way to heal from mental health difficulties related to abuse is to **learn to release**. It does not excuse an abuser, but the victim must learn a new "normal." Even though abuse has taken place, the victim deserves to begin the journey back to freedom. This step is not an immediate solution and takes time. An abuser may have taken a moment or part of the victim's life, but they do not deserve to determine the parts of life not yet lived. A victim ought to love and be loved once again.

Besides abusive life experiences, there are also traumatic life experiences. Although not an exhaustive list, there are some traumatic events that may affect mental health -

Job loss or transition
Death of a family member or friend
Physical injury or disease
Natural disaster
Community violence
Military service
Victim or witness of a crime
Suicide
Financial loss
Divorce or separation
Legal battles

These events can alter the course of a person's life, adversely shifting the mind into overdrive, and cause a mental health breakdown.

FAMILY HISTORY

Every family is dysfunctional. The perfect family is a myth. Loving families exist. Faultless ones do not. This means you observed bad habits and unhealthy environments for the first several years of life. Sadly, what we *observe* is often *repeated*. It is even possible to normalize that which should not be normalized.

Your family, whether you like it, has influenced the person you have become. Mental health can be an observed behavior. If someone in your home spent much of your childhood depressed or anxious, you may be more prone to a similar behavior.

There is **one more** cause of mental health disorders that I chose not to mention in the previous list – *sin or spiritual disobedience*. Why? It is not necessarily a commonly held cause by all health professionals. There may be some readers who are not sure how to define sin so for the sake of definition, sin is *any action, reaction, or thought that opposes God's commandments*. Maybe you would describe your connection with God as complicated. That's okay. All of us have had times of doubt and fear. But I would ask that you take an inventory of your life and invite God back in. Sin separates. Dealing with sin unlocks your connection with God. There is no room here for a comprehensive list of sins; however, consider a few of the 10 commandments from Exodus 20 -

- **Do not have any other god before God** (no person or thing should have priority over God)
- **Do not make yourself an idol** (no image of God should be created to represent God)
- **Do not take the Lord's name in vain** (God's name is not to be taken lightly or misused)
- **Honor your mother and father** (parents treated with respect/honor)
- **Do not murder** (Jesus gave this one deeper meaning by exposing the sin that leads to murder, which is hatred)
- **Do not commit adultery** (Jesus also gave this one deeper meaning by exposing the sin that leads to adultery, which is lust)
- **Do not steal** (do not take something that is not your own)
- **Do not testify or bear false witness against your neighbor** (do not lie)
- **Do not covet** (failure to be content with what we have and desiring to have what others have)

Sin invites mental health struggles into our lives. When we willingly disobey God's commandments and live life our own way, we are living a reality not meant to be lived. Before we move further into the conversation on mental health, we must agree on this truth. **Sin brought disease, decay, and death.**

God did not create us with physical and mental illnesses. When God created the very first human beings (Adam and Eve), He created them free from disease and the breakdown of their bodies; however, their sinful disobedience brought physical and spiritual death.

> "The Lord God took the man and put him in the garden of Eden to work it and keep it. And the Lord God commanded the man, saying, 'You may surely eat of every tree of the garden, but of the tree of the knowledge of good and evil you shall not eat, for in the day that you eat of it you shall surely die.'" (Genesis 2:15-17, ESV)

Adam and Eve had freedom to eat from any tree in the garden except the tree of the knowledge of good and evil. God told them that eating from this tree would cause death. Not immediate death, but eventual death. Adam and Eve disobeyed God. Eve took the fruit and ate from the forbidden tree. Adam also ate and their sin brought the very first taste of sin, guilt, and shame.

When Adam and Eve sinned, physical death did not occur immediately, but they died spiritually. This meant that they were relationally separated from God. The connection between God and man was ruined because of sin. In Genesis 3, the man and woman hid from God. He came into the garden, searching for Adam and Eve, but they had hidden themselves in shame. Adam finally responded to God's calling out to them by admitting that they were hiding because of their nakedness. Before sin, there was no shame in nakedness, but now the relationship between God and man had been broken.

Rather than coming clean about eating from the tree of the knowledge of good and evil, they began to blame each other for their disobedience. Something else significant also began happening. Adam and Eve began to die physically. Each day of life moved them closer to death. We see this process taking place in our own lives. As much as we try to take care of ourselves (physically, mentally, and emotionally), we deteriorate with each passing day.

Have you noticed this pattern in your life? Memory does not get better with age. Aches and pains increase year after year. Strength decreases as a person moves into the later years of life. Although wisdom and maturity may get better with age, your body and mind are breaking down.

There is some good news, though. According to Paul's writing in the New Testament, those who believe in Jesus Christ for the forgiveness of sin have hope of receiving a new body suited for eternal life in heaven. Paul writes about this new body in his letter to the church at Corinth.

> "…For our dying bodies must be transformed into bodies that will never die; our mortal bodies must be transformed into immortal bodies. Then, when our dying bodies have been transformed into bodies that will never die, this Scripture will be fulfilled: 'Death is swallowed up in victory. O death, where is your victory? O death, where is your sting? For sin is the sting that results in death….'" (1 Corinthians 15:53-56, NLT)

Paul's concluding thought is that **sin is responsible for death**. He writes, "But thank God He gives us the victory over sin and death through our Lord Jesus Christ" (1 Corinthians 15:57, NLT). How are we given victory over sin and death? Two-thousand years ago, Jesus Christ came to this earth to give us hope. Since we're separated from God because of sin, we need restoration. Most people believe that trying harder is the key to reconciling with God. However, the Bible is clear that our own efforts cannot bring restoration.

Listen to these truths from the Bible…

> "Salvation is not a reward for the good things we have done, so none of us can boast about it" (Ephesians 2:9, NLT).
>
> "…He saved us, not because of the righteous things we had done…." (Titus 3:5, NLT).
>
> "We are all infected and impure with sin. When we display our righteous deeds, they are nothing but filthy rags." (Isaiah 64:6, NLT).

So, what is the key to being restored to God? Can sin be forgiven?

> "God saved you by his grace *[undeserved favor]* when you believed. And you can't take credit for this; it is a gift from God." (Ephesians 2:8, NLT).

You can be restored to God when you stop trying to earn forgiveness. By faith, you believe that God has opened the door to forgiveness through the work of His Son, Jesus Christ. Forgiveness of sin is a gift. A gift is paid for by the Giver. The one who accepts a gift humbly receives it. Do you need to experience forgiveness? Forgiveness is lovingly and freely available to those who don't deserve it.

Listen to the words of God's prophet, Isaiah.

> "All of us, like sheep, have strayed away. We have left God's paths to follow our own. Yet the lord laid on him the sins of us all. He bore the sins of many and interceded for rebels." (Isaiah 53:6, 12 NLT).

Jesus died and resurrected for those who have strayed far from Him.

Jesus died and resurrected for those who have willingly ignored Him in favor of their own ways.

Jesus died and resurrected for those who have rebelled against Him. God placed your sin on Jesus, and He was crucified on your behalf. God wants to forgive you.

He will forgive you if you receive, by faith, Jesus Christ's death on the cross in your place and believe that His resurrection from the dead brings the assurance of eternal life.

Have you taken this first step in your faith journey? If not, your mental health struggles will not make sense from the perspective of your Creator God. Will you take the first step toward God in this moment by genuinely speaking these words to Him from a broken and humble heart?

Dear God, I know that my life is probably not what it should be. In fact, the standard You have set for me is perfection, which is not something I can attain. Because of my sin, I realize that You are offended and justified in punishing me through physical death and eternal separation from You. I have nothing to offer you but a broken past, attempts at living independent of You, and a trail of sin.

From the beginning of human history, death (physical and spiritual) has resulted from sin and I fully acknowledge that my sins are many and my desires to obey have been few. Even though I may not have the answers to all my doubts, fears, and questions I want to surrender my life to You. I deserve Your wrath on sin. I deserve death to pay the penalty for sin, but You loved me so much that You were willing to send Your Son, Jesus. Instead of putting me to death and being eternally separated from You,

You punished Jesus in my place. The wrath of God was poured out on Him so that I might be forgiven.

I exchange my sin for Christ's perfection. I confess Jesus as my Lord and Savior. I know the story of Jesus did not end with His death, but three days later He was raised to life by the power of God proving Your power over sin and death. Jesus' resurrection is the hope of all who believe in His finished work. As Jesus was physically raised to life and ascended to be with God the Father in heaven, through faith I now have the same hope of a resurrection from physical death and eternal life with God. I may not know You fully in this moment but I commit my life to live in your ways through the power of the Holy Spirit who indwells at the moment of faith. I trust you fully to forgive me and make me right with God. Amen.

Did you just pray those words from your heart in faith? If so, take the next step in telling someone. I'm confident that there are amazing churches in your area, and the people would be overjoyed to know that you have taken this step of faith. You need people who will help you travel your faith journey, especially if a part of your story is struggling with being mentally unhealthy.

If you are having a hard time finding a church (or don't know where to start), you can direct message me on social media and I will help you find a place of worship near you. God does not want us to live in isolation but in relationship.

THINK ABOUT IT

Do you feel guilty about struggling with your mental health? Why or why not?

Are you self-conscious about others finding out that you struggle mentally? Why or why not?

If you have been abused, will you consider telling someone you trust?

What is the biggest mental health struggle you are facing?

For you, does being mentally unhealthy stem from biological factors, life experiences, or family history?

Explain how the first human sin affected mental health.

How would you describe your relationship with God?

CHAPTER 2: FINDING GOD AMID MENTAL ILLNESS

"We long for our bodies to be released from sin and suffering." (Romans 8:23, NLT)

Sticking his finger had become a regular part of Trevor's life since he had been diagnosed with type 1 diabetes as a child. For the first several years after his diagnosis, he didn't mind the extra work and caution of managing the disease. But when Trevor became a teenager, those feelings changed. In elementary and middle school, the other kids thought getting to "make yourself bleed" was pretty cool. But during high school he noticed people staring at him while he was testing his blood sugar at lunch every day. "My body does not make insulin. It's that simple" he thought. "If I don't take insulin, my long-term health could be damaged." Trevor didn't expect people in his high school to feel sorry for him, but it bothered him that they gawked at him. He didn't ask to have this disease. By the time Trevor was a young adult, he had developed a heightened anxiety after a few scary experiences with his diabetes. He was testing his sugar much more than he needed because he was fearful of dying. At first he believed he was just being cautious.

But after several months of mounting stress about his self-care, Trevor realized it was not caution, but an obsession that had taken over his mind. Instead of enjoying life like everyone else in their twenties, a disease he did not ask for had taken him captive. The years of managing his diabetes had left him feeling anxious, depressed, and exhausted. Trevor just wanted to live in a normal body with a normal life. Why couldn't God take away this awful disease and the mental fatigue that it had caused? Trevor did not know how much longer he could endure this.

For those who suffer from disease or long-term sickness, physical health can influence a person's mental health. Enduring a mental or physical health problem is already difficult, but those who face both spend most of their life feeling as if they are missing out. They watch others enjoy each day without having to think deeply about managing their health.

The future hope of a new body and eternal life in heaven is good news to those who suffer from uninvited and unwanted conditions. But how can a person find God amid physical and mental health struggles RIGHT NOW? Unfortunately, being a follower of Jesus does not eliminate life's challenges, temptations, and disappointments. Jesus, before His own death, warned that on "…earth you will have many trials and sorrows" (John 16:33, NLT). The Apostle Paul also wrote concerning the futile desire to rid ourselves of anguish in this life. He said, "…we long for our bodies to be released from sin and suffering" (Romans 8:23, NLT).

You may read these verses and become frustrated by God's lack of a promise to take away every pain. A search through Scripture yields no assurance of vanishing afflictions. Our attention must transition from avoiding a trial, to embracing it. Thankfully, the Bible provides an inside look at how God's people throughout history have embraced trials. The

Bible didn't leave out all the bad stuff. There are many examples of people who struggled through difficulty. Some of those troubles were manifested in the form of mental health.

Elijah, a mighty prophet, spoke on behalf of God. He had just experienced a major spiritual victory against the prophets of Baal (1 Kings 18:1-40), but a woman named Jezebel threatened to kill Elijah because of his victory over the false prophets (1 Kings 19:1-2). Her words put him on edge. Rather than relying on God's power for another victory, Elijah retreated into the wilderness and prayed for God to let him die (1 Kings 19:3-4). Elijah had just witnessed God's power poured out on the prophets of Baal, but his mind was filled with fear. In today's medical language, Elijah may have been diagnosed with anxiety or depression. I'm not downplaying Elijah's failure to involve God in his circumstance, but his real-life context brought him to a place where his feelings and faith did not align. His expectations of himself or God surpassed his experience.

Have you ever considered the prophet **Jeremiah**? He is known as the weeping prophet. Jeremiah was forbidden to marry or have children (Jeremiah 16:2). He knew what it meant to experience loneliness, poverty, and rejection. Jeremiah's vocation was preaching, and he did it for 40 years. Year after year, he called on people to repent and turn to God, but Jeremiah died with little to show for four decades of preaching. People didn't respond to the message he was preaching.

How did Jeremiah react to being in a "dead-end job?" Listen to his own words concerning his value as a human being.

> "…curse the day I was born! May no one celebrate the day of my birth. I curse the messenger who told my father, 'Good news—you have a son!' Let him be

> destroyed like the cities of old that the Lord overthrew without mercy. Terrify him all day long with battle shouts, because he did not kill me at birth. Oh, that I had died in my mother's womb, that her body had been my grave! Why was I ever born? My entire life has been filled with trouble, sorrow, and shame." (Jeremiah 20:14-18, NLT)

Those words provide a window into the mind of Jeremiah. He was in the depths of despair. He was disappointed with life and felt as if his existence was meaningless. Jeremiah's feelings were not just a fleeting moment of disillusionment, but an enduring emotion of dejection. If Jeremiah stopped in to see his counselor, what would be the diagnosis?

One of the most famous examples of someone who faced moments of mental instability was **David, King of Israel**. He wrote words such as the ones found in the Psalms.

> "O Lord, how long will you forget me? Forever? How long will you look the other way? How long must I struggle with anguish in my soul, with sorrow in my heart every day? How long will my enemy have the upper hand?" (Psalm 13:1-2, NLT).

God once referred to David as "a man after My own heart" (Acts 13:22). Although David had cultivated a meaningful relationship with God, it did not insulate him from the highs and lows of life. The Psalms of David are best labeled as a journal of his thoughts, prayers, and feelings. In the Psalms, he often writes of his despair, loneliness, fear of enemies, sinfulness, guilt, and shame. Unfortunately, David also knew what it meant to lose a child. This child was conceived in an adulterous relationship between David and Bathsheba, and we get a glimpse of David's reaction to the child's illness.

> "David begged God to spare the child. He went without food and lay all night on the bare ground. The elders of his household pleaded with him to get up and eat with them, but he refused. Then on the seventh day the child died. David's advisers were afraid to tell him. 'He wouldn't listen to reason while the child was ill,' they said. 'What drastic thing will he do when we tell him the child is dead?'" (2 Samuel 12:16-17, NLT)

Any loving parent, regardless of family dynamic, agonizes when their child is suffering. David was no exception. Pay close attention to the conversation happening amongst David's advisors. Because of David's deep hopelessness over his child's sickness, the concern of his advisors was that he would harm himself if the child died. David was struggling with more than just his child being sick. He had committed adultery. David had a man murdered. David married the dead man's widow. David was confronted by God's prophet about his sin (2 Samuel 12:1-15), not to mention that David was already dealing with the stress of ruling a nation. David was mentally unhealthy because of his own sin. We will discuss the effects of sin and consequences on mental health in a later chapter.

Knowing that some of God's representatives (such as Elijah, Jeremiah, and David) struggled with their mental health gives us tangible and relatable Biblical examples. But how do those of us who live in the present cope with unhealthy emotions and thoughts? Where do we turn when the seasons of despondency overwhelm us?

When I need advice or help, I typically prefer to connect with someone who understands or someone who can relate with my current circumstance. Personally, I believe God used individuals to record their stories in the Bible so those who read it can identify with a real person.

Therefore, many people run to the Psalms when they are worn out, discouraged, or looking for an authentic example. The Psalms are a compilation of prayers, poems, and songs that often express the deepest emotions and feelings of some of God's people throughout history. The words of the Psalms make the reader feel as if they are reading a very intimate journal. David, whom we met earlier, authored many of the Psalms.

Psalm 42 is a journal entry, most likely a song, which pulls back the curtain on someone who desires to experience the joy of worshiping God, but his circumstances have prohibited him from doing so. Let's look at his predicament.

> "Day and night I have only tears for food, while my enemies continually taunt me, saying, 'Where is this God of yours?' My heart is breaking as I remember how it used to be: I walked among the crowds of worshipers, leading a great procession to the house of God, singing for joy and giving thanks amid the sound of a great celebration! Why am I discouraged? Why is my heart so sad? I will put my hope in God! I will praise him again— my Savior and my God! Now I am deeply discouraged… I hear the tumult of the raging seas as your waves and surging tides sweep over me." (Psalm 42:3-5, 7 NLT)

Even though the precise background of this Psalm is unknown, the Psalmist describes his predicament. Some scholars believe King David wrote these words, but we cannot know for sure. What we know is that the writer is in a dark place.

He is crying all day.

He is being harassed.

He is missing the better times of his life.

He fluctuates between highs and lows.

He feels as if he's drowning.

The Psalmist's responses to his trouble are typical signs of being distressed by thoughts and emotions. Let's briefly look at each of these responses.

HE IS CRYING ALL DAY
"Day and night I have only tears for food…"

People typically cry as a response to an overwhelming emotion, whether it be joy or sorrow. Crying allows a person to release their emotions and is an attempt to heal. Have you ever heard people say that they just need a good cry? That's because there can be liberation when someone sheds a few tears. On a spiritual level, consider that God created our bodies. He gave the ability to express emotions. Whatever the writer of this Psalm was experiencing, crying had become a regular part of his daily habit. Depending on a person's threshold for adversity, some individuals are overcome with emotion a couple times a month, so the Psalmist's steady crying was a sign of deep-rooted emotion.

HE IS BEING HARASSED
"...my enemies continually taunt me, saying, 'Where is this God of yours?'"

We live in a society riddled with harassment and bullying. Often the aggressor perceives themselves to be superior to another, which may cause various forms of attack. In the Psalmist's case, he is being harassed verbally. Whatever trial has overtaken him, his provokers have called into question the existence of his God. When his attackers ask, "Where is this God of yours?", it's an assault on his belief system. They are acknowledging the reality of the Psalmist's trouble but have not witnessed God coming to his rescue.

This scenario can be so relatable to those struggling with their mental health. You may know how it feels when someone sees your battle and wonders why God hasn't removed your feelings of anxiety or depression. Their words may cause you to feel as if you are doing something wrong or that God doesn't care about your condition. It's difficult to fight a battle when those standing close by are awaiting your demise.

HE IS MISSING THE BETTER TIMES OF HIS LIFE
"My heart is breaking as I remember how it used to be: I walked among the crowds of worshipers, leading a great procession to the house of God, singing for joy and giving thanks amid the sound of a great celebration!"

This may not be true for everyone's background, but some people with mental health conflicts can look back to better times in life. When current strains seem to be unrelenting, there is almost always a moment or season in the past that was more desirable…a phase when existence didn't seem so exhausting. Suffering intensifies good memories of long-ago.

The Psalmist was lamenting his current circumstance compared to the joys of his past.

He had taken part in worship.

He had led worshippers.

He had sung songs with joy.

He had thankfulness in his heart.

All of it was gone. Rather than celebrating with others, he spent his time in sorrow.

HE FLUCTUATES BETWEEN HIGHS AND LOWS

"Why am I discouraged? Why is my heart so sad? I will put my hope in God! I will praise him again— my Savior and my God! Now I am deeply discouraged…."

I have experienced motion sickness over the last several years. Personally, I blame flying over the ocean for the first time as the onset of that feeling. It has become problematic to ride as a passenger in a car or ride roller coasters. I used to love roller coasters. I spent many childhood summers at Carowinds, a theme park located outside of Charlotte, NC.

When my daughter turned 15 years old, she wanted to go to Cedar Point for her birthday, so I loaded up on motion sickness pills and took her. Cedar Point has some of the best roller coasters in the nation, but many of them are fast, furious and not for anyone who suffers from motion sickness. For the first few hours of the day, I felt like a teenager again…wind blowing through my hair, hands in the air, and loving every minute.

As the day wore on (and my medicine wore off), I began to feel sick. My daughter wanted to ride a coaster called the Wicked Twister. It's basically a U-shaped coaster that reaches speeds of 72mph and thrusts you over 200 feet into the air in a corkscrew motion…backward and forward for what seems like at least 100 times! When the ride ended, I was DONE! I could not handle the ups/downs, highs/lows, and the back-and-forth motion anymore.

Being mentally unhealthy may cause a person to feel like they are teetering between the highs and lows…the back-and-forth of life. In Psalm 42, the writer is literally *preaching* to himself. He moves from discouragement and sadness to convincing himself that his hope should be in God. The Psalmist is not devoid of knowing God's character and capabilities. He verbalizes that his hope is in God, who will eventually come to his rescue. However, he does not see a timely end in sight.

Fluctuating between the highs and lows are not an opportunity for you to lose hope, but to renew it. Never stop fighting against the feelings of hopelessness. God is near, even when you may not sense His presence.

> "The Lord hears his people when they call to him for help. He rescues them from all their troubles. The Lord is close to the brokenhearted; he rescues those whose spirits are crushed." (Psalm 34:17-18, NLT)

His rescue may not be immediate, but His nearness will sustain you until the despondency passes.

HE FEELS AS IF HE'S DROWNING
"I hear the tumult of the raging seas as your waves and surging tides sweep over me."

Of all the Psalmist's responses to his suffering, this might be the most significant. He illustrates his feelings of discouragement in terms of water – *raging seas*, *waves*, and *surging tides*. He feels as if he will drown in a sea of emotions. But upon further examination, please don't miss the word *your*. The writer identifies the "owner" of the waves and surging tides – God. I will give this concept more attention in a later chapter, but our struggles are never outside God's power. He doesn't outsource control. God is intimately involved in our suffering.

Some may interpret God's allowance of sorrow as a character flaw when, in actuality, it is a natural result of man's sin. Sin brought disease, decay, and death. Jesus wants to bring us life. He said, "I have come that they may have life, and that they may have it more abundantly" (John 10:10, NKJV). The abundant life is not a pain-free existence, but a pursuit of peace in knowing Christ.

Most of the remaining pages of this book will focus on the **FIVE ATTITUDES TO BEING MENTALLY HEALTHY**.
1) Peace: The Guarding of Your Heart and Mind (Chapter 3)
2) Patience: The Hope of Your Heart and Mind (Chapter 4)
3) Love: The Strength of Your Heart and Mind (Chapter 5)
4) Confession: The Renewal of Your Heart and Mind (Chapter 6)
5) Comfort: The Testimony of Your Heart and Mind (Chapter 7)

As we examine these chapters, let's remember that the steps to better mental health begin with attitudes, not actions. When something goes awry our initial response is, "What do I need to do?" Rarely, do we ever respond, "How do I need to think?" Proper thinking can lead to appropriate actions.

How do we learn to think properly? Before we answer this question, it is important to understand that these attitudes do not come naturally.

Our default feelings are typically as follows.
Worry rather than *Peace*
Impatience rather than *Patience*
Fear rather than *Love*
Denial rather than *Confession*
Thoughtlessness rather than *Comfort*

The way to peace, patience, love, confession, and comfort is supernatural rather than natural. God can produce these attitudes in those who yield their lives to Him. The word *yield* means to give place to another.

I love driving on highways. Some people avoid them, but there is something wonderful about an unhindered roadway free from stoplights or stop signs. There is one part of the highway experience I dislike – on-ramps. When I'm getting onto a highway, the last thing I want to do is yield to other motorists already in route to their destination. But the law demands that I *yield* or give place to others. *Yielding* brings order and control to what would be an otherwise chaotic driving experience.

Developing these **five attitudes to being mentally healthy** will require yielding your heart and mind to God. In return, He will begin replacing your natural attitudes with His supernatural attitudes.

Embracing the **five attitudes to being mentally healthy** will move us closer to Christ. Along the way, don't expect an instantaneous transformation. For many of us who have struggled with our thoughts and emotions, the battles may never fully subside. But, may we allow these words to be the focus of our hearts and minds.

"Unless the Lord had been my help, My soul would soon have settled in silence. If I say, 'My foot slips,' Your mercy, O Lord, will hold me up. In the multitude of my anxieties within me, Your comforts delight my soul." (Psalm 94:17-19, NLT)

THINK ABOUT IT

What does God say about pain and suffering in this life? Have you fully embraced a God who allows hardship?

Which of the Biblical characters mentioned in this chapter do you relate with the most? Why?

Were you aware of the mental struggles surrounding the people that God used? How does knowing this affect your outlook on your own struggles?

In Psalm 42, David detailed his battle through a tough spot in his life? Which of his actions do you relate with the most and why?

What Biblical attitude do you need to embrace to face the mental health challenges ahead?

CHAPTER 3: PEACE - THE GUARDING OF YOUR HEART AND MIND

> "Do not be anxious about anything, but in everything by prayer and supplication with thanksgiving let your requests be made known to God. And the peace of God, which surpasses all understanding, will guard your hearts and your minds in Christ Jesus." (Philippians 4:6-7, ESV)

FIVE ATTITUDES TO BEING MENTALLY HEALTHY
1) Peace: The Guarding of Your Heart and Mind
2) Patience: The Hope of Your Heart and Mind
3) Love: The Strength of Your Heart and Mind
4) Confession: The Renewal of Your Heart and Mind
5) Comfort: The Testimony of Your Heart and Mind

I grew up with two fun brothers, a wonderful dad, and a saint for a mom. She was stuck with too many males in the house. My dad was relatively laid back, unless you pushed him over the edge. Most of the time, we knew where his line was drawn so we would often stay back a few feet. My youngest brother is the one who had a hard time finding that line. He's the one who spent at least 2 years of his life grounded in his room!

Obviously, my mom was wired differently than my dad. He could stay out of the chaos that often engulfed a home with three boys. Both of my parents loved us very much, but my mom spent a lot of time attempting to establish balance and order to the home. She may have been the very first person to ask, "Can't I just get some peace and quiet!?"

During my teenage years, my brothers and I were obsessed with playing Nerf basketball in the house. If you aren't familiar with Nerf basketball, stop what you are doing right now and search for it online. It's an indoor, mini basketball hoop that hangs over a door and includes a miniature foam basketball. If I had to describe the experience, it is like playing basketball in a living room or bedroom with the same intensity as someone who is playing in a large arena. Somebody will get hurt or break something.

Both of my parents worked full time so there was about an hour and a half gap between the time us three boys arrived home from school and my mom arriving home from work. We filled those 90 minutes with wrestling matches and out-of-control Nerf basketball games. One particularly passionate Nerf basketball game ended with my brother, who will remain unnamed, crashing forcefully into the living room wall. The result? A hip-sized hole in the wall. My parents had repeatedly warned us to settle down the games in the house because something would get broken. I don't recall the consequence of our error in judgment, but those types of missteps usually ended with my mom trying to bring a sense of calming peace back into our home.

Everyone is searching for calming peace - peace in marriage, country, workplace, finances, parenting, and so many other places.

I would describe peace in the following ways –
- Freedom from chaos
- A calm state of mind
- Unity in relationships

The opposite of peace is stress. Stress is a powerful emotional or mental reaction to unfavorable or challenging circumstances. Stress always manifests internally and often leads to an external response. All of us, to varying degrees, know how it feels to keep up appearances…to make others perceive us on our own terms. There is the pressure to succeed or please others. Everyday stresses, such as decision-making or time-management, can be enough to send some people over the edge. Peace is what we ultimately seek, but stress is what we usually find.

Stress typically stems from two thought patterns –
1) The exhausting effort to cause something to change
2) The exhausting effort to keep something the same

Let's examine these thoughts patterns a little closer.

THOUGHT PATTERN #1
THE EXHAUSTING EFFORT TO CAUSE SOMETHING TO CHANGE

This line of thinking says, "I need to get rid of what I have!" Namely, there is an identifiable stress point that should be purged from your life. Allow me to share two examples.

In our society, we have an unhealthy obsession concerning body image. This fascination has instituted a subjective and unobtainable standard of beauty. Media outlets, including social media, keep that standard in front of us every day with images, writings, and even invitations to change our appearance. So, when we look at ourselves in the mirror, we are no longer content and set out to transform the way we look. This pursuit leaves a person exhausted. The fatigue stems from a refusal to be at peace until a certain standard of beauty is attained.

Marriage can bring a sense of companionship and daily support but throw in a few draining seasons and one or both spouses will live in stress. Poor job performance, a muffled spiritual connection, and social withdrawal may be the product of a hectic marriage. Peace may virtually vanish from a once calm relationship. Depression and anxiety may become the new normal. The quest for rediscovering peace is exhausting. In a spouse's mind, peace will not return until there is a certain level of affection.

Both examples reflect a familiar pattern.
...Perceived *Standard*
...Unanticipated *Setback*
...and then Devastating *Stress*

Unfortunately, most of us live in some likeness to this exhausting pattern.

THOUGHT PATTERN #2
THE EXHAUSTING EFFORT TO KEEP SOMETHING THE SAME

This second line of thinking says, "I need to keep what I have!" Not only is it exhausting to rid yourself of an identifiable stress point, but also the struggle in trying to keep everything the same. Most people have a level of comfort and expectation for themselves and others, but over time they discover that those levels are challenged at each transition in life.

My wife and I have two children. They have been an absolute joy in our lives, but we have had our fair share of trials raising them. As they have aged (17 and 19 at the time of this writing), the challenges have become more focused on my wife and I adjusting to their desire for independence. When they were younger, they seemed to need us for everything, and we often wondered if that stage would ever pass. It did. Now that we are on the backside of our children living at home, we wrestle with keeping things the same. Admittedly, this stage of life is difficult to navigate. There is a part of us, as parents, that has built a level of comfort and expectation with our children but shifting seasons will shatter those levels.

The Bible speaks of seasons. Solomon, the wisest person who has ever lived, wrote concerning the extremes of life.

> "For everything there is a season, a time for every activity under heaven.
>
> A time to be born and a time to die.
>
> A time to plant and a time to harvest.
>
> A time to kill and a time to heal.
>
> A time to tear down and a time to build up.
>
> A time to cry and a time to laugh.
>
> A time to grieve and a time to dance.
>
> A time to scatter stones and a time to gather stones.
>
> A time to embrace and a time to turn away.

A time to search and a time to quit searching.

A time to keep and a time to throw away.

A time to tear and a time to mend.

A time to be quiet and a time to speak.

A time to love and a time to hate.

A time for war and a time for peace."

(Ecclesiastes 3:1-8, NLT).

Nothing rarely stays constant. If you spend your life trying to prevent change, your pursuit will end in mounting stress and exhaustion.

The pattern is often the same –
Constructed *Comfort*
Unwanted *Change*
...and then Overwhelming *Confusion*

Part of the struggle to being mentally healthy is the inability to *cause things to change* or *keep things the same*. Ever-changing seasons can leave a person mentally exhausted and void of peace.

After 25 years of marriage, Olivia watched her husband pack the last box and walk out the front door of their once peaceful home. She never imagined that the relationship with her high school sweetheart would end at this time in her life. There was no bombshell issue, but over the last few years she noticed an increasing distance between them. At first, she believed it was a season that every couple experienced, but the last several months of their marriage had been a sea of chaos. The constant fighting and harsh words had caused Olivia to shut down. She had lived most of her life with only occasional hardship, so she was unprepared for such a sudden and profound life-change. The days and months following her husband's departure were filled with unfamiliar emotions, thoughts, and feelings. Rather than turning outward for help and support, she withdrew.

So I want you to put yourself in Olivia's place.

What happens to you in the months following?

Do you learn a new normal?

Do you allow your thoughts to go to dark places?

Will you eventually seek counsel?

Will you ever find peace again?

It's virtually impossible to know how you would respond in this given situation. But your hypothetical response may reveal whether you already have the right tools in place to find peace amid heartache.

If finding peace in this scenario is linked to the *exhausting effort to make something change or keep something the same*, you may never find peace. Why? Because the spouse may never come back. Based on this reasoning, peace is only possible when stressful circumstances change, or anxious feelings subside. Since *making things change* or *keeping things the same* are not sustainable ways to live, you must learn to find peace in the middle of anxiousness and uncertainty. How is this possible? A trade must take place.

Several years ago, I was searching for an office chair. Most normal people would visit their local office supplies store, but I was looking for a specific chair that could not be found in retail establishments. The particular chair I was considering was very costly, so I jumped online and quickly found what I was looking for on Craigslist.

Rather than spending hundreds of dollars on a brand-new chair, I found the same one used and for a fraction of the price. For some of you, even the mention of Craigslist sends you into a panic. We've all read about the bad experiences and dangers of purchasing something from an unknown individual at an unknown location...you know, just using common sense. I share those same feelings, but I have a hard time resisting a good deal.

I emailed the seller, received a kind reply, and journeyed an hour to purchase the item. When I arrived at the seller's residence (more like a compound), it was the shadiest-looking place I have ever visited. I won't bore you with the details but let me just say that it was the perfect place for a murder and subsequent burial of a body. Thankfully, I made it out alive and became the proud owner of a nice office chair.

What is the trade-off in this Craigslist chronicle?

I had to set aside the fear of what *may* happen in favor of what *can* happen.

What may happen focuses on the potential to lose, while *what can happen* focuses on the potential to gain.

Worry cripples and anxiety pushes the pause button.

When we live in the *maybes* of life, fear is the outcome.

Have you allowed fear and anxiety to crowd out the possibility of peace?

The Bible is very clear that someone cannot embrace anxiety and peace at the same time. You must trade anxiousness and worry for the peace of God. The Apostle Paul wrote these essential words to his readers almost 2,000 years ago.

> "…do not be anxious about anything, but in everything by prayer and supplication with thanksgiving let your requests be made known to God. And the peace of God, which surpasses all understanding, will guard your hearts and your minds in Christ Jesus." (Philippians 4:6-7, ESV)

Before you assume Paul wrote those words from the comfort of his home, keep in mind that he was writing from a Roman prison when he penned the book of Philippians. You may even read Paul's words with a shade of cynicism, thinking he lived a comfortable life free from occasions to embrace worry and anxiety. Fortunately, Paul documents his sufferings while writing one of his letters to the church at Corinth.

> "Five different times the Jewish leaders gave me thirty-nine lashes.
>
> Three times I was beaten with rods.
>
> Once I was stoned.
>
> Three times I was shipwrecked.
>
> Once I spent a whole night and a day adrift at sea.
>
> I have traveled on many long journeys.
>
> I have faced danger from rivers and from robbers.

I have faced danger from my own people, the Jews, as well as from the Gentiles.

I have faced danger in the cities, in the deserts, and on the seas.

And I have faced danger from men who claim to be believers but are not.

I have worked hard and long, enduring many sleepless nights.

I have been hungry and thirsty and have often gone without food.

I have shivered in the cold, without enough clothing to keep me warm.

Then, besides all this, I have the daily burden of my concern for all the churches."

(2 Corinthians 11:24-28, NLT)

If anyone is qualified to write about trading worry and anxiety for peace, it is Paul. His life was filled with incidents of abuse, persecution, extreme danger, superficial friendships, exhaustion, long hours, hunger, and stress.

Let's inspect Paul's words in Philippians 4:6-7 and take three steps to trade *anxiousness* for *peace* in our hearts and minds.
Step 1: Remove Anxiety
Step 2: Reveal Requests
Step 3: Receive Peace

STEP 1: REMOVE ANXIETY

"Do not be anxious about anything."

Before we can take this step, Paul's use of the word *anxious* must be explored. As Paul wrote it, to be *anxious* means to be pulled in opposite directions. Regardless of mental health labels (OCD, depression, eating disorders, PTSD, etc.), the unfortunate result is to keep a person moving between healthy and unhealthy thinking. Typically, the mind can distinguish between acceptable and unacceptable thought patterns, but those who struggle with their mental health concentrate on unhealthy patterns. So, when Paul challenges his readers to break the pattern of being anxious, he is telling them to end the "tug of war" in their minds.

Part of the strength in becoming mentally healthy realizes that anxiety does not have to be a way of life. There are two thought patterns—healthy and unhealthy—and choosing which one prevails will determine attitudes, actions, reactions, and outlook. The mechanism for controlling anxiety is not a light switch but a dimmer. Light switches can be turned on and off while a dimmer fades.

I was fortunate enough to know and have a wonderful relationship with all of my grandparents but over the last several years, one by one, each of them has passed away. All of their deaths brought a hard lesson in grief. However, the death of my last surviving grandparent was the hardest. Why? Because I will never have another grandparent. No amount of desperation or despair can bring any of my grandparents back to this life.

As a pastor, there are some bad habits I have learned surrounding death. My frequent encounters with death have resulted in attending dozens of calling hours and performing many funerals throughout my years of ministry.

I have been at bedsides when individuals have taken their last breath.

I've observed disease ravishing a person's body until they live their final moment on earth.

I have watched families cope with expected and unexpected loss, such as miscarriages and the death of a child.

I've seen the young and old alike pass from this life.

Unfortunately, I've also learned to bury my emotions when faced with death. It's as if there is an imaginary light switch connected to my emotions when ministering to a family who has just lost a friend or family member.

I hope to be strong for the family, so I flip my "emotional light switch" to *off*. Although there is some wisdom to balance emotions, I did not expect how this imaginary "emotional light switch" affected my response to the deaths of those in my family. When my last grandparent died, I turned the switch *off*, but I've discovered that the switch eventually gets flipped back on by certain triggers such as memories, past conversations, and experiences.

Instead of viewing emotions and anxieties as either *on* or *off*, we need to treat them as a dimmer switch. A dimmer allows us to control the intensity of the light or darkness.

So how do we view our emotions and anxieties as a dimmer switch?

How do we work through removing anxiety?

The answer is further revealed in the *second step* of trading anxiousness for peace in our hearts and minds.

STEP 2: REVEAL REQUESTS

"...but in everything by prayer and supplication with thanksgiving let your requests be made known to God."

Anxiety dims when a person prays. Prayer seems a little confusing, especially if God already knows all things. Why pray when God comprehends every worry, stress, and anxiety? Is prayer a tool to get God's attention so He will know how deep the struggle runs? Without prayer, does God remain unengaged and uninformed? Let's think a little deeper about who benefits from prayer.

God is not necessarily the benefactor when prayers of anxiety are offered. He desires to hear and answer prayer but doesn't necessarily receive anything in return.

Anxious prayers typically benefit the one who is talking to God through authentic and heartfelt words. In its truest form, the prayers of anxiousness are an act of dependence. When someone prays the words *help me because I'm anxious*, they are inviting Him into their struggle. Rather than attempting to live independent of Him, anxious prayers are an admission that *I need God*.

Paul uses two words to describe the communication of anxiousness to God: *prayer* and *supplication*. The word *prayer* carries the idea of directing words at God. *Supplication* is to identify a very specific need to God. God is not ignorant of stress or worry but speaking specific needs to Him allow a person to release control into the hands of an all-knowing and all-powerful God.

Carol and Keith had been married for over three decades, but they were facing one of the biggest challenges of their lives – sick and aging parents. Carol's mom had recently died after a long battle with breast cancer. The difficulty of the disease and the aftershock of her death had left the entire family exhausted, unprepared, and unsure about how to care for her dad. Both Carol and Keith were still working full-time jobs and had been trying to help their recently divorced daughter and her two young children.

Decisions had to be made on how to care for her father. Although he needed a little extra care, he refused to transition into an assisted living care facility. Carol was not only struggling through grief but also guilt. She was a follower of Jesus and believed the words written by the Apostle Peter, "…casting all your anxieties on him, because he cares for you" (1 Peter 5:7, ESV); however, she was not sure how those words could apply to her situation.

She was convinced that God cared about her circumstances but did not know how He would show His care for her. Carol's grief and guilt led her down a path of total despair and discouragement. The grief over her mom's death was so heavy and the guilt about putting her dad into an assisted living facility was too much to endure.

How does Carol cast her anxious feelings of grief and guilt onto God and find strength to make wise and compassionate decisions?

We find the key in the word *casting*, which conveys the idea of throwing something. Carol's grief and guilt must be thrown to God. Every time these thoughts raise their ugly head, Carol must immediately name them before God and give her feelings over to Him.

Rather than holding grief and guilt in her hand, she throws them to God. She transfers her anxieties to Him. Is letting your *requests be made known to God* and *casting all your anxieties on Him* a onetime occurrence? No. Those who are prone to anxious thoughts or feelings of deep despair must practice throwing them to God. Making requests known to Him gives you the opportunity to invite God into your struggle. He doesn't leave you alone in your time of need. He's right there.

Tell Him your request right now. God is listening. Prayer comes before peace.

STEP 3: RECEIVE PEACE
"And the peace of God, which surpasses all understanding, will guard your hearts and your minds in Christ Jesus."

When an individual is working through *removing anxiety* and *revealing their anxiousness to God by prayer*, God can then give peace. Peace is not the absence of pain or suffering but God's supernatural ability to guard the heart and mind. It is interesting that the Apostle Paul singles out the *heart* and *mind* in times of anxiety. He knows that they are most affected by worry.

The heart is the part of us that loses hope. The mind is the part of us that loses stability. God's peace brings hope where hope is lost. God's peace brings stability where there has been instability. Lasting peace is not found in you or in your relationship with another person. This peace, the kind that transcends all human understanding, is found when you invite God into your struggle and live in complete dependence on Him no matter what obstacles you face.

You may expect God to change the *circumstance*, while God expects to change *you*.

What if your particular struggle in the mind does not go away? Can a person find peace? The Apostle Paul pulls back the curtain of his own struggle with a situation that appeared to be out of his control. He writes about an unknown difficulty that he faced regularly.

Paul had seen God do some amazing things throughout his life. He had been given supernatural visions and revelations by God, which were beyond human understanding. In 2 Corinthians 12, Paul was writing about one of these visions where he had been given a personal tour or glimpse of heaven. This experience had the potential to result in pride, so God allowed something into Paul's life that kept him humble.

> "So to keep me from becoming conceited because of the surpassing greatness of the revelations, a thorn was given me in the flesh, a messenger of Satan to harass me, to keep me from becoming conceited." (2 Corinthians 12:7, ESV)

There has been plenty of speculation about the identity of Paul's *thorn in the flesh*, but the *ESV Study Bible* provides four potential explanations.

> **(1)** Paul's inner psychological struggles (such as grief over his earlier persecution of the church, or sorrow over Israel's unbelief, or continuing temptations). **(2)** Paul's opponents, who continued to persecute him. **(3)** Some kind of physical affliction (possibly poor eyesight, malaria fever, or severe migraine headaches). **(4)** Some kind of demonic harassment.[v]

It is particularly thought provoking to consider that Paul's struggle could have been psychological. Regardless of the identity of Paul's *thorn in the flesh*, it affected him to where he begged God to take it away. Paul believed he could be more effective *without* the thorn than *with* it. Paul even says, "Three times I pleaded with the Lord about this, that it should leave me." (2 Corinthians 12:8, ESV). Paul wanted the struggle to go away.

Did God take it away? No.

> "Each time he said, 'My grace is all you need. My power works best in weakness.' So now I am glad to boast about my weaknesses, so that the power of Christ can work through me. That's why I take pleasure in my weaknesses, and in the insults, hardships, persecutions, and troubles that I suffer for Christ. For when I am weak, then I am strong." (2 Corinthians 12:9-10, NLT)

Unfortunately, we often believe our lives will function better in the absence of weakness.

We dream of a life free from mental health struggles.

But what if they are the very things that keep us dependent on God?

What if the things that expose our anxieties are the very things that have the potential to keep us near to God?

What if freedom from anxiousness would bring about a life lived in pride?

Peace is not tied to changing circumstances but an unchanging God. He has promised supernatural peace where natural peace cannot be found.

God's strength begins with our weakness.

THINK ABOUT IT

Is the direction of your life characterized by peace, lack of peace, or no peace? Why?

What person, thing, or situation is causing the most stress in your life?

Is it possible to have peace in the middle of mental health battles?

Which of the following thought patterns are making you void of peace: the exhausting effort to cause something to change or the exhausting effort to keep something the same?

How can you apply Paul's writing in Philippians 4:6-7 to your current thought patterns?

CHAPTER 4: PATIENCE - THE HOPE OF YOUR HEART AND MIND

> "I waited patiently for the Lord; he inclined to me and heard my cry. He drew me up from the pit of destruction, out of the miry bog, and set my feet upon a rock, making my steps secure." (Psalm 40:1-2, ESV)

FIVE ATTITUDES TO BEING MENTALLY HEALTHY
1) Peace: The Guarding of Your Heart and Mind
2) Patience: The Hope of Your Heart and Mind
3) Love: The Strength of Your Heart and Mind
4) Confession: The Renewal of Your Heart and Mind
5) Comfort: The Testimony of Your Heart and Mind

When I graduated from college with a degree, I had this distorted idea that it would only take a short time to find a job in my field of study. In the second semester of my senior year, I began sending out resumes and confidently awaited job offers to roll in. I quickly discovered that finding the right job took time, follow-up, and determining whether I fit into a particular opportunity. There was one job in particular that I desperately wanted because it fit **my** timeline and the path I had created for **my** future.

If I'm being honest, the job would speed up my marriage date. You can't blame a guy for wanting to get married sooner than planned!

That job opportunity (as I had imagined it in my head) began to fall apart and it left me with nothing. I was angry. It ruined all **my** plans. Marriage would have to wait a whole year and I would spend the next twelve months miserable because **my** timeline did not work out the way I intended.

Admittedly, it is easy for me to look back, nearly 25 years later, and see that it was better for **my** plans and **my** timeline to be spoiled. I ended up marrying my wife (a year later than I wanted) and earning a graduate degree, which was not in my original plan. What I did not realize is that the begrudged *pause* in my life eventually made sense. God ultimately provided an amazing job at the right time. If I had attempted to make my initial plan and timeline work out, I may have spent a few years trying to get back on track.

Although God worked things out better than I could have imagined, I still hate waiting. There are three L's that test my patience every single time – *Lights*, *Lines*, and *Life*. When I see a red stoplight ahead, I will search for ways to keep moving…even if that means slowing down or turning down another street. I also cannot stand waiting in line. Somehow, I always choose the wrong checkout line. I could select a line with one person in front of me, but the line beside me with ten people will move faster. It's maddening!

I also struggle with waiting in life. I want what I want right now. In my twisted opinion, *waiting* means to miss something or suffer a setback. A delay in progress or lack of forward motion makes us believe that we are losing at life or lagging behind everyone else. In our limited assessment, waiting delays the enjoyment of life, overcoming obstacles, and developing maturity. But is this really the truth? Is *waiting* the enemy?

> A common theme among some who wrestle with mental health is that they equate joy with the fulfillment of self-imposed timing and demands.

If a goal is not accomplished, or a feeling is not shaken in a pre-determined amount of time, a person can become disheartened. It is even possible for the attitude of impatience to bleed into our view of God. We give Him ultimatums and question His love or goodness when His timing does not match our timing.

But who gets to determine how long is too long?

To answer that question, let's take a journey back into the Old Testament book of Psalms. Psalms is unique in all of Scripture because it is a compilation of lyrical poems written by multiple authors. Out of 150 Psalms, David wrote nearly half. Reading some of them feels almost intrusive because of the personal nature of the writings. Several of David's Psalms make the reader feel as if he has found someone's intimate journal. What makes it more awkward is that David does not hold back his feelings of God's abandonment or silence. Modern-day churches have conditioned us to keep those type of feelings quiet, but David wrote his feelings and millions of people throughout history would know he struggled to understand God's timing.

In Psalm 40, we do not know the exact situation that resulted in David recording these words, but we know it can be divided into two parts.

Psalm 40:1-10 recalls a past struggle, while Psalm 40:11-17 refers to a current one. An ordinary reading of these verses would suggest that David is preaching to himself. He was thinking back to a time when God delivered him and hoped that He would do the same in his current situation. Let's examine a couple of truths extracted from this Psalm concerning patiently waiting through trials.

Here is the first truth.

PATIENTLY WAITING DURING TRIALS IS NOT AN ISSUE OF <u>IF</u> GOD WILL SHOW UP, BUT <u>WHEN</u>.

"I waited patiently for the Lord; he inclined to me and heard my cry. He drew me up from the pit of destruction, out of the miry bog, and set my feet upon a rock, making my steps secure." (Psalm 40:1-2, ESV)

David describes his past circumstance as being in a *pit of destruction*, a *miry bog*, and a place without stable footing. He was not describing a literal place, but a frame of mind and whatever had befallen him caused him to face a seemingly hopeless situation. It is the place many of us retreat when life has backed us into a corner with no visible escape.

Lisa had a stable job handling the finances for a growing company. She had been with them since two business partners took a risk and launched the endeavor four years ago. No one expected how quickly they would flourish, but Lisa had enjoyed seeing the business start from scratch and become a place of employment for nearly 100 people. In the early days everything seemed a lot simpler even though the hours were long, and the pace moved fast. She relished in the company's success and the satisfaction of the employees. While she was getting ready to leave for the day, one of the founding business partners stopped into her office and closed the door. He asked her to make a few slight changes on the financial reports to make the company appear a little more profitable to the investors. When he walked out of her office, Lisa felt an overwhelming sense of conflict in her heart. On one hand, she wanted to be loyal to her boss, but she also knew that the guilt of lying would not be something she'd be able to handle long-term.

After a sleepless night she went into work the next day and told her boss she did not feel right about falsifying the financial packet that was being distributed to current and potential investors. Her decision set in motion months of misery. Lisa's relationship with her boss completely changed, and he worked behind the scenes at destroying her credibility. Instead of responding to the lies that were being told about her, Lisa hung on and hoped things would eventually settle down. Her husband had recently lost his job, and they had two kids who needed the financial stability her job provided. A year passed, and the situation had only gotten worse. Lisa struggled to keep it together. She had been praying that God would resolve the problem and had even asked a few of her close friends to pray for her strength. With each passing day it became harder to get out of bed and go to work because she did not want to face the continual whispering going on behind her back.

You may not relate with Lisa's exact situation, but you may know what it feels like to find yourself in a *pit of destruction* by no fault of your own. You have prayed. You have begged God to step in, but He hasn't intervened in the way you asked. During these times of painful silence, you have asked God, "How long?"

David's past struggle does not have a timeline on it, but eventually he was delivered out of the *pit* and *bog*. How did David position himself while waiting? He waited *patiently*. As I have stated already, I am not questioning the severity or legitimacy of your struggle, but those struggling with staying mentally healthy must learn to wait patiently. The words *waited* and *patiently* both mean looking toward something with anticipation.

Rather than questioning **IF** God will arrive to deliver you from your difficulty, anticipate **WHEN** He will show up. The timing is not important if you know God is on His way. Although it is tough to patiently wait, realize that you are only viewing the circumstance from one viewpoint – your perspective.

Throughout my life, I have been fortunate enough to travel to many countries. One place I have visited more than once is Mexico City, Mexico. Each trip has allowed me to fall in love with the people and places in Latin America. But while I am traveling in unfamiliar countries (no matter the location), I feel as if I have lost all control. Each twist and turn takes me to locations with which I am unaccustomed.

On one particular trip to Mexico, I was leading a group of 30 individuals, most of them in high school. It was a lot of responsibility. Near the end of our trip our group visited a large, outdoor marketplace which was one highlight of our journey. After several hours of journeying through the seemingly endless alleyways, all of us boarded the bus and headed to our next destination. About 15 minutes after we left the marketplace, I discovered that a student was missing from the bus and most likely had been left behind. You can imagine the fear that immediately came over me.

In that moment of panic, my heart wanted nothing more than to get that individual back where they needed to be, but I knew it would not be soon enough. The 15-20 minutes it took for a couple of the locals to hop out of the bus and take a taxi back to the marketplace probably seemed like an eternity to the person alone in an unfamiliar place.

What was one of the biggest obstacles to overcome in this situation? Time. I knew that there were people on their way to rescue this student, but each second that the individual was alone most likely brought about the question in their mind, "Are they coming back for me?" I knew my heart and the heart of our leaders was for a rapid rescue, but every passing minute of aloneness created an uncertainty in the student's mind.

This frightening event was never a question of **IF** we would go back and find this high-schooler. We loved and cared for every person in our group, including the one who was alone in this moment. The greater issue was **WHEN** because it is nearly impossible for a person in a *pit* to view the situation from the perspective of the One who is watching over them.

Although God does not *cause* harm, He *allows* it. He may allow you to experience the awful things that tag along with our mental health. These struggles are not meant to push you away from God but to Him. Has your despair and discouragement pushed you away from the heart of God? If so, you may need to gain a greater understanding that patiently waiting for God draws us closer to Him.

And, here is the second truth discovered in patiently waiting on the Lord.

PATIENTLY WAITING FOR RESCUE DURING TRIALS MAY BREAK YOU DOWN, BUT THE LORD WILL BUILD YOU BACK UP.

"He put a new song in my mouth, a song of praise to our God. Many will see and fear, and put their trust in the Lord." (Psalm 40:3, ESV)

Suffering through tangible anguish often leads to mental unhealthiness, which has a way of breaking a person down…way down. Sometimes the breaking down leaves an outer shell with little left on the inside. If David found himself in a pit of destruction where he had lost all footing, all of us can identify with his fight-or-flight response.

But while David is in this pit, it exposes us to what he was clinging to. When a person is in a pit, it implies that there are no footholds to escape; otherwise, they would have already made their way out a long time ago. So, when there is nothing to cling to, where does an individual turn? Where did David turn? This Psalm reveals that David prayed and in His own timing the Lord set his feet on a rock. God does not allow suffering for the sake of suffering. There is always a divine purpose. This means in the middle of any struggle, there should be a confidence that God will build back up.

God does not allow His children to fall apart so He can leave them in a pile of despair and discouragement. He takes that heap of disappointment and creates something new with the pieces that were once broken. In David's case, God put a "new song in his mouth." In the original language of this Old Testament Psalm, the word *new* does not mean words that had never been spoken. The word *new* carries the idea of familiar words being spoken with a fresh meaning.

It is irrefutable that trouble changes a person. In fact, your mental health struggles are not a weakness to be resented but an opportunity for you to showcase God's goodness, strength, and power. The byproduct of David's time in the pit of destruction was that he could be an example of what can happen when an individual waits on the Lord. His words in this Psalm are not *first* words, but *fresh* words. Because of his stint in the pit, David could look at life with God in a fresh, new way.

As God delivered David out of this circumstance, there was an anticipation that he may help someone else glimpse the Lord through it.

David viewed what we could perceive as a weakness as a way for others to see God, fear Him, and even put their trust in Him.

> "He put a new song in my mouth, a song of praise to our God. Many will see and fear, and put their trust in the Lord." (Psalm 40:3, ESV)

If you're in a pit and have no foothold, have confidence that God will eventually set your feet on stable ground and give your circumstance a platform to help others see God amid their conflict. And that platform is only given when you have been where someone else is.

What God allows to fall apart, He will build back up.

To some, reading these words may seem like nothing more than a motivational speech that will end in more mounting disappointment. You are right. There is no protection from climbing out of one pit only to fall into another. In fact, this is David's story. In Psalm 40:1-10, he was recounting one pit while entrenched in another pit, which you can read about in Psalm 40:11-17.

There is no easy solution while you are patiently waiting in the pit of destruction. If you are worn out and cannot find a foothold, allow the prayer of David's heart to be the prayer you declare until God arrives.

> "As for me, I am poor and needy, but the Lord takes thought for me. You are my help and my deliverer; do not delay, O my God!" (Psalm 40:17, ESV)

In this moment, proclaim these three statements -
God, I am in need.
God, I know You are my helper and deliverer.
God, please show up soon.

…and remember that it is not about you convincing yourself **IF** God will show up, but **WHEN**. And when He shows up, He builds up what has been broken down.

So, patiently wait.

THINK ABOUT IT

What self-imposed timeline or expectation is causing your mental health to suffer?

In your current struggle, can you find the value in waiting?

How can you change your current perspective from wondering <u>if</u> God will show up to anticipating <u>when</u> He will show up?

Can you see the potential for God to use your pain for your good and the good of others? Why or why not?

Explain how God can build up what has been broken down in your life.

CHAPTER 5: LOVE - THE STRENGTH OF YOUR HEART AND MIND

> "For I am sure that neither death nor life, nor angels nor rulers, nor things present nor things to come, nor powers, nor height nor depth, nor anything else in all creation, will be able to separate us from the love of God in Christ Jesus our Lord." (Romans 8:38-39, ESV)

FIVE ATTITUDES TO BEING MENTALLY HEALTHY
1) Peace: The Guarding of Your Heart and Mind
2) Patience: The Hope of Your Heart and Mind
3) Love: The Strength of Your Heart and Mind
4) Confession: The Renewal of Your Heart and Mind
5) Comfort: The Testimony of Your Heart and Mind

So far on our journey through the attitudes to being mentally healthy, we have examined the attitudes of peace and patience. We do not find *the attitude of peace* in changing circumstances but embracing a God who is unchanging. He has promised supernatural peace where natural peace cannot be found. God's strength begins with our weakness.

The attitude of patience is discovered by understanding that mental health struggles should not cause us to question **if** God is present in our pain. He is always there but sometimes His timeline for rescue is not the same as ours. No matter how long we wait for God to help us endure our battle, He will build up what may have been broken in a moment of collapse.

The third attitude to being mentally healthy is the *attitude of love*. Although most would agree that love is best displayed through action (and it is), love begins with an attitude. Love in action without love as an attitude is hollow. Rather than trying to understand the attitude of love through a concept, we will uncover love through closely examining God Himself – *His help in weakness, His working all things together for good, His gift of Jesus,* and *His refusal to abandon us.*

Before discovering God's love in attitude and action, let's acknowledge love's relationship to mental health. Love has the potential to make a person experience happiness or joy. Love sometimes can help an individual better manage stress or anxiousness. Love can even make people more determined to take care of themselves.[vi]

But a lack, absence, or loss of love can easily turn each of these outcomes upside down. Happiness turns to sadness. When love is unfulfilled, the capability to handle stress may cause anxious living. The diligence to take care of oneself can vanish when no one is present for accountability or purposefulness.

The difficulty in human love is that it is always with risk. There are no guarantees that the extent of love given or received will remain stable. If this is true, people spend most of their lives on a mental health seesaw – controlled by the ups and downs of love. While every person experiences the highs and lows of love, it can crush those with mentally unhealthy patterns under the burden of wavering affection.

Entering middle school is an awkward time for most kids, but Brittany was arriving into the sixth grade with a few more pounds than her classmates. She was a little self-conscious, especially when she compared herself to the other girls in her class. When Brittany confided in her mom about how she was feeling, her mother told her not to worry because she would grow into her weight. Her mom's advice seemed to suffice until a boy in her class made a comment about her size. It devastated Brittany. For the next several years her weight fluctuated, and she found herself more and more unhappy with the way she looked in the mirror. Brittany thought, "If I don't love the way I look, no one else can love me either."

In Brittany's first year of college, she was exposed to how some other girls maintained their weight…by making themselves sick or skipping meals. At first this reality upset Brittany, but she began to realize that most of the young girls who were doing this had boyfriends.

In the months ahead Brittany began skipping meals and noticeably lost weight. When Brittany returned for her sophomore year of college, she was down 40 pounds and fitting into clothes that she never imagined possible. One of the senior guys in her literature class began to take notice of her and asked Brittany to go out for dinner. She could not contain her excitement over this potential relationship and attributed this development to her newfound outlook on her body image.

One date eventually turned into a long-term relationship with the guy in her literature class, but what Brittany did not realize is that she had mistakenly equated love and acceptance with a number on the scale. Controlling her weight became Brittany's coping mechanism whenever she felt fat, stressed-out, fearful, or unloved. Brittany's view of love was no longer rooted in a settled way of thinking (attitude), but a set of actions.

The potential to give or receive love can cause us to take drastic actions; however, love should never begin with action but an attitude. Love that begins with action is almost certain to change when the action changes. But love that begins with attitude has the potential to remain stable through changing actions.

Brittany's belief system about love now included a self-imposed body image. If she looked a certain way, then she would be capable of giving and receiving love. Unfortunately, when Brittany's relationship fell apart, so did her view of love. In her mind, she had taken the right actions to secure a relationship, but it was her unhealthy attitude toward love that led to its demise.

In the human realm, there is no such thing as perfect love, which often sends a person's mental health into an unsafe decline. So, the conversation we are about to engage in is very important to being mentally healthy. **God loves His followers perfectly in attitude (the way He thinks about us) and action (the way He acts toward us).** This truth should cause us to find our stability in Him, not in whether we give or receive love with other human beings. Please do not misunderstand me. God desires us to love and be loved, but a proper view of love begins with the way He thinks about and acts toward us.

In Romans 8, the Apostle Paul writes concerning the longing that every follower of Jesus should manifest – to be redeemed. This means that those who believe in Jesus know this life is tough and exhausting, but

God has promised an eternal life without suffering and pain. Although this should provide a present and future hope, it still does not remove the worries of this present life. It is into this very tension that God steps in to show His love in attitude (what he thinks about us) and action (the way He acts toward us).

Let's consider ***FOUR WAYS GOD DEMONSTRATES HIS LOVE FOR US IN ATTITUDE AND ACTION.***

GOD'S LOVE IS DEMONSTRATED IN HIS HELP IN WEAKNESS

> "Likewise the Spirit helps us in our weakness. For we do not know what to pray for as we ought, but the Spirit himself intercedes for us with groanings too deep for words. And he who searches hearts knows what is the mind of the Spirit, because the Spirit intercedes for the saints according to the will of God." (Romans 8:26-27, ESV)

No one is a stranger to weakness…not even the one who follows hard after Jesus. God knows that. He knows your struggle. He knows your worries. He knows your stresses. He knows your mental exhaustion. How are these weaknesses displayed? By not knowing how to pray as you should.

Have you ever been so weak – mentally, physically, emotionally – that you couldn't even come up with the words to say to God? If you have been in a mentally unhealthy place, you *know* what it is like to be void of words to express your feelings to God. You move your lips, but no words are spoken. Most know what it is like to be in a strained dialogue and struggle to find the words to express the way you feel. That is frustrating for both people. One is trying to communicate, and the other is attempting to understand. Usually, a one-sided conversation does not end well. Both leave discouraged.

It is different with God because He loves you even in your weakness. *Instead of turning away from you, He turns toward you.* At the moment you cannot find the words to communicate your frailty to God, He prays on your behalf. **It should be an overwhelming truth that God prays for you.** I've had many people pray for me throughout my life, but there are no prayers comparable to God's. His prayers on your behalf are valuable because no one knows the will of God like God Himself. In your moment or season of weakness, God knows the plans He has for you and can pray on your behalf better than you. Rest in that.

How does God think about you? He has chosen the attitude of love despite weakness.

How does God act toward you? He prays for you when you do not know how to pray for yourself.

GOD'S LOVE IS DEMONSTRATED BY HIS WORKING ALL THINGS TOGETHER FOR GOOD

> "And we know that for those who love God all things work together for good, for those who are called according to his purpose." (Romans 8:28, ESV)

Before further discussing this second demonstration of God's love, there must be some honesty and transparency about the complex nature of this truth. But just because this is a challenging truth does not mean it should be avoided. What makes this truth so puzzling? It is hard to understand how **God can use what we interpret as *bad* for *good*.** You may look at being mentally unhealthy as an undesirable part of your life, but it may be that very struggle which keeps you dependent on God.

The human instinct drives people to rid themselves of any obstacle that might cause pain or suffering, but sometimes God allows conflict to remain for our good, the good of others, and ultimately the glory of God. The *good* may not be immediately known or perceived, but those who love God can be confident He is at work even in what they may perceive as *bad*.

> "In his providence, God orchestrates every event in life - even suffering, temptation, and sin - to accomplish both our temporal and eternal benefit." – John MacArthur [vii]

Calvin grew up in a loving and supportive Christian home. It was always a little tight with money, but his parents always provided Calvin and his siblings with their basic needs. When Calvin graduated from high school, he knew they would not have the money to help him fund his education, so he joined the military.

Adjusting to life as a soldier was no easy task, but Calvin began to thrive and quickly climbed the ranks. Instead of pursuing a college education, he enlisted for 5 more years. The benefits and stability were unmatched. In his fourth year of military service, Calvin was deployed overseas, which changed him forever. He witnessed many atrocities, but none worse than seeing one of his best friends lose his life in a surprise attack. Calvin was devastated about losing a good friend and even more shattered that he had to continue on with "normal" life.

This incident set in motion a series of feelings and emotions that Calvin did not realize lived inside him. The last year of his enlistment was a struggle. He tried to do what he thought was right – attend chapel services, see a counselor, and keep himself busy. When his 5-years of service was up, Calvin returned to civilian life so he could hopefully find a new *normal*. The first few months provided a needed escape from his feelings and emotions. He spent time with his friends and family while also beginning a college education. Since college was his first choice anyway, he thought it would offer an outlet to find a renewed purpose. As the newness of being home wore off, Calvin found those angry and frightened feelings returning. Small things would set him off. He was easily startled, and his awareness of his surroundings was heightened. He began to turn inward. Others started noticing that he was not himself and encouraged him to get help. After a few sessions with a counselor, she told him that what he had seen and heard while overseas had caused the ongoing feelings of trauma. This was no surprise to him. The counselor he had seen while in the military had diagnosed him with PTSD (post-traumatic stress disorder). Labeling the feelings was meaningless to Calvin. He wanted solutions. How would he ever resume a normal life? Calvin's story is not uncommon. Soldiers are returning from active duty every day trying to fit back into civilian life. Most people do not fully understand what military women and men have observed during service for their country.

Attempting to apply the *God working all things together for good* truth in this situation proves difficult. In fact, if you've experienced any trauma – abuse, natural disaster, life-changing accident, or violence – it is problematic to apply this truth. It almost sounds flippant when something unimaginable occurs and we speak words such as "God will bring good from what seems bad" or "God has a plan for your pain." Although these words may be true, they make God emerge as cold, uncaring, or absent.

We find the solution in balancing God's love in attitude and action. At the center of pain and suffering is man's sin. When we examine traumatic events, many of them are carried out because of the dreadful nature of mankind and the natural consequences of a decaying universe. God never intended *bad*, but man chose to live independent of God and brought miserable hurt upon himself and others. Since God's attitude toward human beings is to redeem and restore, His actions are to work all things together for good to them that love God. He takes what others meant for evil and uses it for His highest good.

How does God think about you? He has chosen the attitude of love despite mankind's evil ways setting in motion the consequences of sin.

How does God act toward you? He makes all things, including bad, work together for good.

GOD'S LOVE IS DEMONSTRATED BY HIS GIFT OF JESUS

> "What then shall we say to these things? If God is for us, who can be against us? He who did not spare his own Son but gave him up for us all, how will he not also with him graciously give us all things?" (Romans 8:31-32, ESV)

When a person is in the middle of a battle with their mental health, it is easy to feel the weight of the world pressing in, as if everything and everyone is against them. Depression and despair often lead an individual to withdraw and refuse to receive help.

Aubrey had just given birth to her second child. Having another baby was an easy decision since Brandon, her firstborn, had been such an agreeable infant. She had heard horror stories of babies who cried all day and refused to sleep through the night. Her fingers were crossed that Maya, her newborn, would be as cooperative as Brandon. The first few weeks were uneventful, but then Maya began having a difficult time keeping anything down. This led to a lot of crying and sleepless nights for both Aubrey and her newborn. She had already paid a visit to the pediatrician, researched natural remedies online, and received advice from the moms at her church. Nothing seemed to work. Aubrey's husband was very supportive, but he spent most of the day at work since they heavily depended on his overtime pay. Weeks turned into months and Aubrey found herself in a place of despondency. All she wanted to do was sleep and forget everything. She had reached the point of rejecting any help. No one met the needs of Maya, so Aubrey quit receiving offers for help. She felt like a failure compared to all the other moms. They seemed to have it together and could keep their babies happy and healthy.

Some may say that Aubrey's hopelessness is not relational and relevant to deep spiritual matters; however, Satan and his evil system within the world spend a lot of time wreaking havoc in people's lives through ***discouragement***. When a person feels discouraged, they often consider themselves less useful for the purposes God has intended, maybe even unlovable by Him. The comparison game is prevalent in the world. It's everywhere.

Consider your occupation. Who is it you are always trying to "beat out?"

Consider your marriage. Whose relationship looks so perfect that it makes you nauseous to even be around them?

Consider your financial status. Who causes you to burn with envy and jealousy?

Consider your singleness. Who makes you feel less than enough because of your relational standing?

Consider your body image. Who do you hate seeing because they seem to be perfect?

Consider your connection with God. Who makes you seethe with anger because it appears they have it all together while you are falling apart?

Comparison to others is a dangerous game that you will never win and ultimately leads to discouragement. It triggers a person to journey down a path that often makes them feel unloved and unwanted. Discouragement is one of the biggest enemies to being mentally healthy because it causes one to question their worth. The key to battling discouragement is understanding that worth is not determined by what you have or haven't done, who you are or were, or how you do or don't compare to others. Your worth is determined by *what God thinks about you* and *how He has acted toward you.*

Paul reminds his readers in Romans 8:31-32 that God went to great lengths to show the extent of His love for mankind by sending His Son, Jesus Christ, to save people from their sins (Matthew 1:21). God sent Jesus to seek and save those who are lost (Luke 19:10). God sent Jesus for those who are spiritually sick (Luke 5:31). Paul reveals that God's love and our worth are confirmed by Him giving the gift of His Son, Jesus, to show how far He will go to rescue and renew.

> "Satan and his demonic hosts are against believers, but they cannot ultimately prevail and triumph over believers. God is the self-existent One and the sovereign Creator and, since He is for believers, no one can oppose believers successfully. He is for believers to the extent that 'He ... did not spare His own Son, but gave Him up for us all.' ...In view of this supreme act of God's grace, How will He not also, along with Him, graciously give us all things? Since God gave the greatest Sacrifice of all, His own Son, He will certainly not hesitate to give believers all

other things pertaining to and leading to their ultimate sanctification." [viii]

How does God think about you? He has chosen the attitude of love even when we do not measure up compared to others.

How does God act toward you? He gave the gift of His Son, Jesus, to show the worth and value of the one who believes.

GOD'S LOVE IS DEMONSTRATED BY HIS REFUSAL TO ABANDON HIS FOLLOWERS.

> Who shall separate us from the love of Christ? Shall tribulation, or distress, or persecution, or famine, or nakedness, or danger, or sword? No, in all these things we are more than conquerors through him who loved us. For I am sure that neither death nor life, nor angels nor rulers, nor things present nor things to come, nor powers, nor height nor depth, nor anything else in all creation, will be able to separate us from the love of God in Christ Jesus our Lord. (Romans 8:35; 37-39, ESV)

Anxiety, depression, or many other mental health disorders can force a person to alternate between *wanting to be alone* and *not wanting to be alone*. Anxious thoughts may bring you to the place where you do not want anyone near, but there are other times you need people near. It's difficult to discern this thinking pattern, but it is equally difficult for friends and family to navigate your swings between isolation and nearness. When the pendulum is swinging back and forth, it is vital to reach past your *feelings* to the *facts*. Your *feelings* tell you that you've been abandoned or want to be abandoned. The *facts* are that God's love compels Him to remain with you through all of your ups and downs. Nothing can separate you from the love of God in Christ.

Abandonment can even affect those deemed as spiritual leaders. Consider these thoughts written by the pastor of a small church in Delaware.

> Yesterday, I spoke to a half empty sanctuary. I felt like no one was really engaged with what I was saying, but maybe they were, and it was just me whose heart wasn't into it. Because I've been a pastor for many years, I know the right things to say but I can't decipher how to make my heart believe what I'm saying. I used to feel so confident in my faith. That was when my faith fit into my desired expectations and predetermined outcomes. It's different now.
>
> Making my feelings match my faith has proven to be the greatest battle of my life. I'm supposed to be the one who is strong for everyone else - my family, my congregation, and the people who trust me.
>
> Who do I run to for strength? Who lifts me up when I can't seem to motivate myself to make it through the next 24 hours?
>
> I strangely identify with the guy in Scripture who cries out to Jesus, "I believe, but help my unbelief." I can't remember where that story is in the Bible, but that's how I feel…like I want God to be there, but don't really know if His presence is making a difference.
>
> Can belief and unbelief co-exist?

If so, that's where I am. I believe in God, but I don't know if I believe in all His ways. I believe He is near, but He feels so far away. I don't know if it's me who abandoned God or if it was Him who left me alone.

Let us consider Paul's question in Romans 8:35, "Who shall separate us from the love of Christ?" He then gives three scenarios where we may be tempted to believe that we could become detached from Christ's love - *tribulation*, *distress*, and *persecution*. All three words are highly relational to what a person may face in remedying their doubts about God's love and healthy thought patterns.

TRIBULATION

This word carries the idea of any hardships common to all people from being in a relationship with God and experiencing normal, everyday life. It may be the tendency of one who struggles with mental health to question God's love when circumstances do not unfold in their favor. Paul is writing to let his readers know that trials do not change the way God feels about you. He loves you even when things around you seem to be falling apart.

DISTRESS

This term refers to a person being in a position where escape may seem hopeless. In my experience, distress has always been one of my biggest struggles. When I can see the light at the end of the tunnel, I narrowly avoid feelings of anxiety; however, when there does not appear to be a way of escape, I shut down. God wants us to know that His love remains the same even when we encounter an overpowering hopelessness. God does not abandon in times of distress.

PERSECUTION

Paul is referencing a questioning of God's love when others seem to be against us. Most of us know how it feels when unjustified attacks result in discouragement. Paul reminds his readers that assaults from an adversary may cause temporary harm, but He has not left us alone.

How does God think about you? He has chosen the attitude of love when life does not go as planned.

How does God act toward you? He will never abandon you in time of need.

God's deep love for His people leads Him to take action on their behalf. He promises that He will *help in our weakness*, *work all things together for good*, *make the gift of Jesus available*, and *refuse to abandon us*.

THINK ABOUT IT

How would you describe the depth of giving and receiving love? Have your thought patterns prevented you from experiencing love in the way God meant for His people to experience it?

Describe what it means to you that God prays on your behalf when you do not have the words to say. What does this show about God's love for you?

Do you believe God is working all things together for good? If so, what areas do you need to believe that truth?

What does the gift of Jesus mean for those who receive Him by faith?

If nothing can separate us from the love of God, how should that affect the way we think about our mental health?

CHAPTER 6: CONFESSION - THE RENEWAL OF YOUR HEART AND MIND

> "I acknowledged my sin to you, and I did not cover my iniquity; I said, 'I will confess my transgressions to the Lord,' and you forgave the iniquity of my sin." (Psalm 35:5, ESV)

FIVE ATTITUDES TO BEING MENTALLY HEALTHY
1) Peace: The Guarding of Your Heart and Mind
2) Patience: The Hope of Your Heart and Mind
3) Love: The Strength of Your Heart and Mind
4) Confession: The Renewal of Your Heart and Mind
5) Comfort: The Testimony of Your Heart and Mind

Sometimes being mentally unhealthy directly results from sin and disobedience in your life. Although it may sound harsh to insinuate that your mental health struggles can be of your own choosing, it is the truth. Some mental health disorders are easily explained because of patterns or instances of sin throughout your years of living. I want to carefully draw the line, so there is not a misunderstanding. If you have disobeyed God's ways and are experiencing the natural consequences of sin, the way back to being mentally healthy is through confession. What is confession? Confession is an acknowledgement of wrongdoing before God and others, intending to turn from sin and walk in obedience. It is not just a guilty feeling for getting caught but an actual brokenness for offending God and others.

Confession is the key to unlock the door to being mentally healthy once again. For some reading these words, the most critical action in regaining healthy thought patterns is to return to the place of your sin, confess it before a holy and righteous God, and then move in a new direction. Abandon the path you are walking for the better path – God's.

Liam and Shannon had been married for seven years. Shannon's dad was the pastor of the church where Liam's family had been attending for decades. Liam and Shannon were high school sweethearts and just carried their relationship right over into the Christian college they attended. The first five years of their marriage were filled with young love and adventure, but Shannon's recent miscarriage had sent her into a deep depression. When she first lost the baby, she clung to her husband and found solace in his understanding and compassionate care. But over the last six months Liam had been trying to move past the heartbreak while Shannon was still struggling through the loss. Liam had exhausted all the "things" he was supposed to do, and he was frankly at a loss. Since he and Shannon had stopped talking about the situation (it just led them further apart), Liam began talking to Jocelyn, a young woman in the office next to him. She listened. She didn't judge. She offered an outlet for Liam to speak what he was feeling. She made him feel seen and heard once again – just like Shannon did before the miscarriage.

Liam began spending a little more time in Jocelyn's office and they even went to lunch a few times. They just enjoyed each other's company. After Liam and Jocelyn's friendship had deepened, he dreaded going home to Shannon. After Shannon would fall asleep, Liam and Jocelyn would text into the early morning. Liam could not wait to get to work each morning. It was a place of refuge and escape from the cloud of hopelessness that hung over his own home.

The owner of the company assigned Liam and Jocelyn to a new client that had the potential to be lucrative for the business, but it required them to stay late a couple nights during the week. Most of the time, they were the only ones left in the office. This extra time together only brought their friendship to a new level. They worked hard together. They laughed together. They were accomplishing something together. The rejuvenated feelings of purpose and meaning made Liam question whether he would ever be happy with his wife, Shannon. Jocelyn complimented his skills and lifted his spirits. Shannon only seemed to bring him feelings of unhappiness. Liam began thinking he had made a mistake in marrying Shannon. Maybe she wasn't his soulmate.

Then it happened. On one of the late nights Liam and Jocelyn were alone in the office, he kissed her. He immediately felt guilty, but he enjoyed it and knew that she also did. This kiss set into motion a series of decisions that Liam began to justify in his mind. He made excuses and did his best to convince himself that the highest aim in life was to be happy and Jocelyn was making him the happiest he had ever been. Shannon had only brought him misery, at least that is what he had convinced himself to believe. He considered it Shannon's fault for making him seek companionship in another woman.

After a month of what seemed like a dream come true, Jocelyn suddenly ended the affair with Liam. It shattered him. Jocelyn told Liam that she felt guilty about what they were doing and needed to break it off to have a clear conscience once again. Losing the connection and companionship of Jocelyn sent Liam into a downward spiral. The last several months with Jocelyn had been some of the best in his recent memory and now she was gone. In his mind, Liam blamed Shannon. It was her fault. Her emotional and physical absence was not fair to him. Liam withdrew and became very disheartened. He lost motivation, slept more, and did not feel any fulfillment in life. When he was at his lowest point, he scheduled an appointment with a psychiatrist. Liam explained how he was feeling but left out all the details about his affair with Jocelyn. The psychiatrist labeled him as depressed and prescribed a couple medications to help take the edge off of the way he was feeling. Even though the medications would most likely help Liam feel a little better, the root issue was not the depression but the sin of his affair. Medication was an attempt to relieve the guilt and shame that could only be remedied by acknowledging his sin before God and making things right with his wife, Shannon.

Allow me to be very clear. When there is unconfessed sin at the root of a mental health struggle, the first step is making things right with God and others. Medication or counseling, by itself, will not relieve the guilt and shame of the natural consequences of sinful choices. Wise counsel and, potentially, medication can help in a person's journey to healing; however, looking inward and dealing with sin is vital. Masking sin hides reality and does not move a person in a direction of restoration.

If your lies and deceitfulness are making you feel anxious, confession is the first step to becoming mentally healthy once again.

If your gossiping and slander has caused you to lose relationships and feel depressed, confession is the first step to becoming mentally healthy once again.

If an overwhelming desire for control and manipulation is causing obsessive-compulsive behaviors, confession is the first step to becoming mentally healthy once again.

In this moment…right now…ask God to reveal any areas of your life that are being lived contrary to His ways. If anything is brought to mind through the conviction of the Holy Spirit, stop what you are doing and confess your sin to God.

Let's dive a little deeper into how you and I can deal with our past and present sins to move forward in living a life of being mentally healthy.

Confession and restoration are definitely not a formula, but I want to provide some action steps to take in renewing your relationship with God…
- Receive God's forgiveness through Jesus
- Confess your daily sins to God
- Reconcile quickly with others
- Move on

RECEIVE GOD'S FORGIVENESS THROUGH JESUS

Although the words written here about confession are important, no one can fully understand confession until they have entered a relationship with God and experienced His forgiveness. How does a person know if they have a relationship with God and have been forgiven by Him?

At the beginning of human history, God created Adam and Eve (Genesis 1:26; Genesis 2:8-25) and placed them into the Garden of Eden where they enjoyed perfect companionship with Him. They were given freedom in the garden to eat of any tree except the tree of the knowledge of good and evil (Genesis 2:15-17). If they disobeyed God's commandment and ate from the tree, they would experience physical death and eternal separation from God (Genesis 2:17). After listening to the lies of Satan (a fallen angel), Eve and eventually Adam disregarded God's commandment by eating from the forbidden tree (Genesis 3:1-13) and their disobedience brought the consequence of sin, death, and eternal separation from God upon the entire human race (Romans 5:12).

Much like Adam and Eve, you have sinned by disobeying God's commandments. Even the person who thinks of himself as good and moral has broken God's law (Romans 3:10-12) by doing things such as dishonoring their parents, hating, lusting, stealing, and lying.

Before you weigh your good and bad works, remember that Adam and Eve were sentenced to death because of a single act of rebellion. Therefore, if you have only sinned once, you are guilty before a holy and righteous God (James 2:10). Whether your sins are many or few, you must be punished for sin through death and eternal separation from God (Romans 6:23). Good works cannot satisfy God's prescribed punishment for sin. "For the wages of sin is death…" (Romans 6:23, NLT).

Is there any hope of forgiveness for those who have sinned? Because Adam and Eve disobeyed, God promised that from the woman's seed (offspring) He would eventually bring into the world a Savior to defeat the works of Satan and destroy sin and death (Genesis 3:15). How would this be accomplished?

This Savior would be punished on behalf of the sinner. He would be put to death on a cross for sins He did not commit so that the sinner could be set free (2 Corinthians 5:21). Nearly 2,000 years ago God sent His only Son, Jesus Christ, into the world to set mankind free from the penalty of sin and offer eternal life to anyone who would trust in the sacrifice of His Son.

> "For God made Christ, who never sinned, to be the offering for our sin, so that we could be made right with God through Christ." (2 Corinthians 5:21, NLT).

Although Jesus died for the sins of mankind, He did not stay in the grave. Three days following His death, Jesus was raised to life by the power of God (1 Corinthians 15:1-4), but in the same way He was resurrected from the dead, those who believe in Jesus Christ's death for sin and His resurrection, will be given eternal life (1 Corinthians 15:20-22).

According to God's divine will and plan, forgiveness of sin cannot be earned. Forgiveness is a gift (Romans 6:23) offered to anyone who will put their faith in the death and resurrection of Jesus Christ as the payment for their sin.

Maybe you feel unworthy. Maybe you feel as if your sins are too many or too extreme. The Apostle Paul clarifies that no one is beyond forgiveness. Here are the words he writes in Romans 10:9-10,13 (NKJV)...

> "If you confess with your mouth the Lord Jesus and believe in your heart that God has raised Him from the dead, you will be saved. For with the heart one believes unto righteousness, and with the mouth

confession is made unto salvation. For whoever calls on the name of the Lord shall be saved."

Anyone who calls out to God and puts their faith in the finished work of Jesus Christ (His death for sin and resurrection) will be saved from the power and penalty of sin. We have used many words to describe the forgiveness available through the sacrifice of Jesus Christ; however, listen to these simple words from the Gospel of John...

> "For God so loved the world that He gave His only begotten Son, that whoever believes in Him should not perish but have everlasting life. For God did not send His Son into the world to condemn the world, but that the world through Him might be saved." (John 3:16-17, NKJV)

God's love for mankind led Him to send His Son to die for the sins of men.

Will you receive His love and forgiveness through trusting in Jesus' death for sin and His resurrection as the assurance of eternal life? If you will, God receives You as His child. A proper relationship with God is imperative to taking the next steps.

CONFESS YOUR DAILY SINS TO GOD

We like to talk about the past. Well, that statement is only half-true. We are inclined to discuss the good memories and forget about the bad ones. It's much easier to relive accomplishments, successes, and happy times while doing our best to ignore inabilities, failures, disappointments, and sin. Our trophies are on display for everyone to see, but our shame is hidden away. We have become experts at hiding things, especially what we do not want others to discover. Here is the problem with this thought pattern.

You cannot hide the past from yourself.

No matter how hard you work at tucking the past away, it always has a way of resurfacing. Why do shameful parts of our past reappear? The answer is simple. Guilt and shame return when the sins that mark our past have not been properly handled. Rather than facing our sin, we bury it in a shallow grave. There are many dangers in concealing past sin, but here are two of them.

Unconfessed sin negatively affects our relationship with God and others
The writer reminds us that "People who conceal their sins will not prosper…" (Proverbs 28:13, NLT). There can be no prosperity in life for those who hide their sins.

Unconfessed sin affects our well-being
We are also told by the writer, "The wicked run away when no one is chasing them…" (Proverbs 28:1, NLT). Since the past still haunts those who have done wrong, they always believe someone will find them out. Are you living in fear of being found out? If there are hidden sins in your past or present, they must be handled properly. Choosing to keep them hidden away will cause them to resurface at the most unusual times.

So, what do we do with what we have already done since there are no do-overs in life? We cannot relive expired days and moments. We cannot retract spoken words and actions. Once in a lifetime opportunities have vanished. Sinful deeds are now a part of our story. There is so much finality to the past that often leads to ongoing feelings of guilt, shame, and regret. How would you feel if your past sins could be erased? What if the sin and shame that taints your past could be removed from your record?

You can be released from your sin. The apostle John writes the following words to believers in the first century...

> "But if we confess our sins to him, He is faithful and just to forgive us our sins and to cleanse us from all wickedness" (1 John 1:9, NLT).

Forgiveness of sin is based on whether you will agree with God about your wrongdoing and take responsibility for your sinful thoughts, attitudes, and actions. When David's sin of adultery and murder was discovered (see 2 Samuel 11-12; Psalm 32; Psalm 51), he prayed these words –

> "Finally, I confessed all my sins to you and stopped trying to hide my guilt. I said to myself, 'I will confess my rebellion to the Lord.' And you forgave me! All my guilt is gone." (Psalm 32:5, NLT)

At the heart of his prayer of confession, David offered advice to the godly who found themselves guilty of sin.

> "Therefore, let all the godly pray to you while there is still time, that they may not drown in the floodwaters of judgment." (Psalm 32:6, NLT)

The first step in dealing with sin is confessing it to God. Confession is not just feeling guilty, but a genuine heart of sorrow and brokenness over sin. **IF** you confess, God will forgive. Forgiveness is conditional.

RECONCILE QUICKLY WITH OTHERS

Does confession mean that a situation is over? Yes, and no. When your sin is a private matter, confession before God is enough; however, when a shameful part of your past involves another person, there must be an attempt at restoring that relationship. Making things right with God is the first step but making things right with others is the next step. A person cannot properly worship God until they have attempted to reconcile with someone they have sinned against.

> "So if you are presenting a sacrifice at the altar in the Temple and you suddenly remember that someone has something against you, leave your sacrifice there at the altar. Go and be reconciled to that person. Then come and offer your sacrifice to God." (Matthew 5:23-24, NLT)

Jesus' teaching is very clear. Worship of God is unacceptable until there has been an attempt to resolve a conflict with someone else. Did you leave a job with unresolved issues? Have you refused to speak with a family member because of a past argument? Did your relationship end with unresolved issues?

If the answer to any of these questions is *yes*, true confession cannot be set in motion until you attempt to reconcile with the person you have offended. Unresolved conflict with another person will always be a part of an unresolved past until you have sought restoration. There is no way to sidestep this requirement.

What if you approach a person in humility, but they refuse to forgive you? When you approach another individual with the right heart attitude, but they reject your attempt to make things right, the responsibility now rests with them. You cannot force someone to reconcile. The situation must then be entrusted to God so He can be free to work in their heart.

There will never be a convenient time to make amends, but it is a necessary step in properly dealing with sin. Do you need to reconcile with someone? Make the phone call to apologize. Write the letter of confession. Schedule a conversation to ask forgiveness.

MOVE ON

If you have confessed past sins to God and have sought reconciliation with the people from your past, then why do you have a difficult time forgiving yourself?

It's sometimes easier to receive God's forgiveness than it is to forgive yourself. Maybe it's because we still live with the consequences of our sin. Or maybe it results from being disappointed in ourselves.

What makes this more confusing is that the Bible never really speaks concerning "forgiving yourself." So, a follower of Jesus doesn't really have a reference point...or do they?

Although the Bible never specifically mentions forgiving ourselves, the Bible provides many examples of people who moved on with their lives after shameful sins. The past is the past. You cannot change it no matter how much you beat yourself up. If you grieve every single day for the sins of your past, it still won't change what you have already done. Remember that Jesus Christ paid the penalty for your sin so you could be released from the power and penalty of sin.

Please listen to this. It's time to move on. You cannot change the past, but you can change today and tomorrow and the next day.

Adam and Eve brought sin upon the whole human race (Genesis 3; Romans 5:12).

Noah brought shame on his family when he got drunk and naked in his tent (Genesis 9:18-29).

Sarah suggested that her husband, Abraham, have sex with her servant so they could have a child to call their own (Genesis 16) …so he did.

Moses murdered an Egyptian (Exodus 2:11-15) and later in his life refused to do what God asked him to do (Exodus 3-4).

Israel, God's chosen people, repeatedly turned their backs on Him and worshipped other gods (too many occurrences to list here).

David, King of Israel, committed adultery and conspired to murder the woman's husband (2 Samuel 11-12).

Solomon had it all but was never satisfied (Ecclesiastes).

Jonah refused to obey God and later pouted because God allowed people to be forgiven.

All of Jesus' disciples abandoned Him during one of the hardest moments in His life (Matthew 26:56).

Peter, one of Jesus' closest friends, denied that he even knew Him (Matthew 26:69-75).

Saul, who later became Paul, persecuted and probably even killed Christians (Acts 8:1-3).

These real-life people in the Bible did some very shameful things, but they all had one thing in common - they had to move on. ***There is NO excuse for their sin***, but they had to move forward with life. Some of their stories ended well. Some of them did not.

My advice to you is this…
Receive God's forgiveness through Jesus Christ.
Confess your daily sins to God.
Reconcile quickly with others.
Move on.

I know you may be ashamed of what you've done, but it will be more shameful if you waste the rest of your life wishing to change the past…which cannot be fully erased. Forget what you cannot change so you can free yourself for the plans God has in place for you.

THINK ABOUT IT

It's time to get honest. Are there sins in your life that could potentially cause your struggles with mental health? If so, how will you respond to your sin?

Do you have a relationship with God – not just a surface belief in God, but a relationship where you have trusted Him with your whole life and live to follow in His ways? What does that relationship look like daily?

What relationships are broken in your life, and how will you attempt to restore them?

Explain the consequences of continuing to ignore your sin.

Have you confessed your sin before God and made it right with others? If so, how have you felt it difficult to forgive yourself?

CHAPTER 7: COMFORT - THE TESTIMONY OF YOUR HEART AND MIND

> "Blessed be the God and Father of our Lord Jesus Christ, the Father of mercies and God of all comfort, who comforts us in all our affliction, so that we may be able to comfort those who are in any affliction, with the comfort with which we ourselves are comforted by God." (2 Corinthians 1:3-4, ESV)

FIVE ATTITUDES TO BEING MENTALLY HEALTHY
1) Peace: The Guarding of Your Heart and Mind
2) Patience: The Hope of Your Heart and Mind
3) Love: The Strength of Your Heart and Mind
4) Confession: The Renewal of Your Heart and Mind
5) Comfort: The Testimony of Your Heart and Mind

Our journey has taken us through four of the five attitudes to being mentally healthy. Each attitude has challenged our thinking, which will prayerfully change our actions. These attitudes are not developed overnight but over time as we give the Holy Spirit control over all parts of our lives, including thought patterns. Nurturing our mental health is a daily struggle between what is *felt* and what is *fact*. Some lies we believe keep us in holding patterns that move us away from healing and trapped in dangerous places. The reality we have discovered along this journey is that our fight against being mentally unhealthy may never go away. Therefore, our hope should not be in a changing circumstance, but in developing healthy attitudes toward ourselves and the One who created and loves us.

In this last attitude to being mentally unhealthy, I want to take us to a place that may leave us with more questions than answers. This discussion may overthrow some ways we view God. Chasing this thinking may uncover a greater purpose to our struggles than we ever imagined, but it is an uncomfortable conversation to begin. It will force us to release selfishness in our mental health and look upward and outward.

Here is the deep question.

What if God allows you to struggle with mental health so your story and testimony can help others?

Stop here if you read that question without stopping to deeply consider the answer. Allow me to ask it another way. Can physical or mental suffering be for the glory of God and the good of others? We have already discovered that He works all things together for good to those who love Him (Romans 8:28). Amid this suffering God will bring glory, fame, and attention to Himself; however, your pain also has the potential to comfort others. We cannot always decipher *why* God allows something to happen, but we can be certain *what* He will do with it – bring *glory* to Himself and comfort to others.

There is a little story tucked away in the gospel of John that you rarely, if ever, hear about in church. Two-thousand years ago in Jesus' culture and country, people with physical disabilities or mental instabilities were looked down upon. The community often ostracized them. The judgment of these individuals was rendered because of people questioning the genuineness of their spirituality. The crippled, blind, speech-impaired, or mentally unstable were considered spiritually broken by the people who lived nearby. Those attitudes have not changed much in the last two millennia, but the language has shifted. Those with a physical or mental illness are considered "less than" and accused of not having enough faith to overcome a particular battle. This philosophy has soaked deep into the roots of the 21st century church. In this belief system, they treat God like a divine genie who does what we want Him to do if we ask in deep faith. The inherent danger of this notion is that control and sovereignty is managed by us, not God. God becomes a passive bystander who does what we tell him to do. Instead of being Lord, He is your assistant. This viewpoint questions whether God should have the ability to allow ongoing suffering if it benefits His glory and is for our good.

Look at how this thinking permeated the community of Jesus and even His own disciples.

> "As Jesus was walking along, he saw a man who had been blind from birth. 'Rabbi,' his disciples asked him, 'why was this man born blind? Was it because of his own sins or his parents' sins?'" (John 9:1-2, NLT)

Even Jesus' closest followers (His disciples) had adopted the shallow thinking of the culture. They assumed that the man without sight had been born blind because of a sin he or his parents had committed. It is improper for us to assume or speculate *why* God allows physical or mental illness in a person's life. The disciples would quickly learn that their belief system was flawed. Jesus responded to His disciples' assumption by answering, "It was not because of his sins or his parents' sins.... This happened so the power of God could be seen in him" (John 9:3, NLT). It is unfathomable to us that God occasionally allows suffering for no other purpose than to put His supremacy on exhibit so that people would know and believe there is a God in heaven. How did God put His power on display? Check out the rest of the story.

> "Then he spit on the ground, made mud with the saliva, and spread the mud over the blind man's eyes. He told him, 'Go wash yourself in the pool of Siloam' (Siloam means 'sent'). So, the man went and washed and came back seeing! His neighbors and others who knew him as a blind beggar asked each other, 'Isn't this the man who used to sit and beg?' Some said he was, and others said, 'No, he just looks like him!' But the beggar kept saying, 'Yes, I am the same one!' They asked, 'Who healed you? What happened?' He told them, 'The man they call Jesus made mud and spread it over my eyes and told me, Go to the pool of Siloam and wash yourself.' So I went and washed, and now I can see!'" (John 9:6-11, NLT).

I love happy endings, but there is something in me that wishes to point a finger at God and ask for a deeper explanation. This man was born blind and because of the culture he lived in, they considered him an outcast. He resorted to begging to make ends meet. I assume someone had to take his hand every day and lead him to the place where he would sit and beg. Or maybe he stumbled his way from an alleyway, where he slept, into the streets to hold out his hand to receive something from people who looked down upon him. This does not sound like fairness. This does not sound like a good God. But this is where our belief system is flawed. We mistakenly believe that *we* are the center of God's world, but it should be *He* who is the center of ours. It seems scandalous to suggest that God's plans are higher than our pain. "This man's blindness was not caused by some specific sin. Instead, the problem existed so that God could display His glory in the midst of seeming tragedy." [ix]

I do not know for certain, but I guess that receiving sight did not take away this man's future problems. New pain probably replaced old pain, but now he would have Someone to hang onto. He had a story. He had a testimony. In fact, we get to hear him share it with these simple but profound words, "I was blind, and now I can see!" (John 9:25, NLT)

Later on Jesus found the former blind man and asked, "Do you believe in the Son of God?" (John 9:35, NKJV) and the man answered saying, "Who is He, Lord, that I may believe in Him?" (John 9:36, NKJV). The man once blind was not sure if Jesus was only a good prophet or the Son of God, but He revealed His true identity to this man by declaring, "You have both seen Him and it is He who is talking with you" (John 9:37, NKJV). The man who had been healed of his blindness immediately responded to knowing Jesus' true identity by saying, "Lord, I believe!" and then he worshiped Him (John 9:38).

Spiritual healing is greater than physical healing. It's convenient to be physically and emotionally healthy, but spiritual health sustains and gives us Someone who will never leave or forsake us. When you are walking through the valley of despair, He is there.

It is comforting to know that God makes Himself known to us during suffering, but there is a second way we should view our mental health struggles. **God comforts us so we can comfort others**. In the first century, the Apostle Paul wrote some powerful words to the church in the city of Corinth. They carry a principle that is just as relevant today as it was when they were first written.

> "Blessed be the God and Father of our Lord Jesus Christ, the Father of mercies and God of all comfort, who comforts us in all our affliction, so that we may be able to comfort those who are in any affliction, with the comfort with which we ourselves are comforted by God." (2 Corinthians 1:3-4, ESV)

The *Bible Knowledge Commentary* provides some insight to these verses.

> "Troubles, Paul said, help Christians shift their perspective from the external and temporal to the internal and eternal. The source of all comfort in the midst of troubles is God Himself, to whom Paul gave three titles: the Father of our Lord Jesus Christ, the Father of compassion, and the God of all comfort. This same God had sustained Paul through his suffering and delivered him from it. Just as spiritual gifts are not intended solely for the recipients' benefit but are to be used in turn for the service of others, so comfort received from God enables believers to comfort others. The comfort of God is channeled through people and by means of prayer." [x]

I don't intend to assign guilt to those who barely have the mental strength to make it through the day; however, I want to challenge you to think beyond yourself to how God might use *bad* for *good*. Your mental health struggles, in God's plan, have a deeper purpose than just learning how to get through another day. God wants to comfort you so you can comfort others. The prayer of the mentally unhealthy needs to not only include "help me make it through today" but also "help me help someone else make it through the day."

If you know what it means to spend years struggling through a deep depression, ask God how He can use it to comfort someone else.

If you experience mental health struggles from past abuse, ask God how He can use your story to bring hope to others.

If you have struggled through an eating disorder or addiction, ask God how He can use your insecurities and pain to deliver others out of their season of despair.

If you experience PTSD, ask God how your story of trauma can move people from brokenness to hopefulness.

At some point, personal *struggle* must turn to personal *testimony* because a *silent* struggle is a *wasted* struggle.

The extent of your influence might not be hundreds or thousands of people. The number is not important. It is important, though, that you open your eyes to the individuals already in your life. Who could benefit from hearing your story? Who needs the same comfort that you have already received from God?

Preston lay flat on his back, looking up at his bedroom ceiling. He didn't know how long he'd been there, and he really didn't care. He rested in this moment of joy. Even though his journey had been full of heartache and sin, He could see God's faithfulness. It had not always been this way. As a recent college graduate, Preston thought life would lighten up after he completed his degree and jumped into the workplace. The last twenty years of his life had been spent in some kind of formal education, so he was happy to land a job as an accountant. For the first few months, he felt out of place because most of his co-workers already had a couple years of experience. Once Preston settled into his new position, he looked forward to going to work each morning. He even started hanging out with some of his co-workers after work. Although they grabbed a few beers to wind down after a hard day, seeing other people drink brought back agonizing memories for him. Preston had taken his first drink at a party when he was 14 years old, which led him to a struggle with addiction.

When Preston entered his sophomore year of high school, he also began experimenting with drugs. Preston believed he was in control until he wasn't. On his way home from his school prom he crossed over the double yellow line and was involved in a head on collision with a mom and her two children. All he remembered was crawling out of the shattered passenger window of his overturned car and hearing the screams of a woman. Preston knew he had had too much to drink and swallowed some pills his friend had given him.

When he woke up the next day, he discovered that both children had been ejected from the other car and it paralyzed one of them from the waist down. The other child suffered a traumatic brain injury that resulted in seizures and slurred speech. There was a chance that neither child would ever be the same. In the year following the accident, Preston spent time in a juvenile detention center where he was disciplined as a minor and given time to learn about the consequences of his decisions. While Preston was in that detention center, he began attending a weekly Bible study led by a local pastor. At first, he went because he felt like he needed to make up for ruining the lives of the mom and two children but as time went on Preston began understanding God's forgiveness.

Before they released him, he had a face-to-face conversation with Amy, the mother of those two children. He poured out his heart and asked for her forgiveness. She looked him in the eyes and said, "I will never forgive you. You have ruined my life. You have ruined my children's life. You have ruined my husband's life. We will never be the same." It crushed Preston. He thought Amy would respond differently when she saw how he had changed and wanted to make things right with her. That was the last opportunity Preston had to speak with her. During his freshman year of college, Amy took her life. She had slipped into a deep depression and saw no other way out. Her husband, Connor, was left alone to take care of their two children. Preston carried a huge burden with the knowledge of this news. He felt like his bad decision had ruined the lives of this family, and probably countless others.

During college, Preston found a local church to connect with and began growing in his faith. What began as a childlike faith in a juvenile detention center grew into a maturing faith as he formed some deep relationships with a group of guys. These men prayed for and invested in Preston throughout his time in college. When he opened up about how he had ruined a family's life, his group of friends helped him understand how God could heal his broken heart. By the time Preston graduated from college, he was sharing his story in local high schools and churches to warn about the impact of wrong choices. Even though he could not go back and change what he had done, he felt as if he was experiencing some amount of redemption by warning students to make wise decisions. Preston was aware of his failures but was also thankful for how far God had brought him.

There had been a growing desire in Preston's heart to make amends with Connor, Amy's husband. He knew it was a longshot considering how she had reacted to him many years ago. Through a series of connections, Preston met face-to-face with Amy's husband. Connor was very kind and forgiving. It overwhelmed Preston. He felt like part of the burden he had been carrying around since he was 16 years old had been lifted…nearly ten years later. This wasn't the last conversation between Preston and Connor. An unlikely friendship developed, and God began to work in both of their hearts about how He could use this tragedy for good. Over the next year Connor and Preston's unusual friendship caught the eye of the local media and they did a story about forgiveness and redemption.

As Preston lay on the floor of his bedroom staring at the ceiling, he was overcome with emotion. The twists and turns in his life had often made him question the value of his life, but God now allowed him to look back and see His faithfulness through the mess.

Preston and Connor's stories originate from different places. Preston's story allowed him to receive comfort from a local pastor in the juvenile detention center and the guys at his college church. The comfort did not come because something was done to him, but because he had done something to someone else. Connor's comfort did not come because he had done something to someone, but because something had been done to him. Oddly enough, Connor experienced comfort by allowing God to turn his anger, depression, and anxiety into a story of redemption and forgiveness. As God had comforted both men, they were now using the power of story to comfort those who were experiencing difficult circumstances. Each time they spoke at a school or church, dozens of people would line up to express how Preston and Connor's story had inspired them to forgive.

Both Preston and Connor struggled through extreme mental battles that pushed their minds to the edge. Neither path was easy to travel, but both individuals got to experience God's comfort and then put it on display for others to find comfort in their pain.

God never promises a life free from emotional suffering, but He promises to comfort those who invite Him into the difficulties of life. And when they have experienced the supernatural comfort from God, they cannot resist making sure others know the power of this comfort. No matter which side of comfort you are on – comfort through the forgiveness of sin or comfort through the fear of suffering – there will always be an opportunity to make much of God's love and forgiveness.

The choice is yours. Your mental health battles can stay locked away in your mind or you can throw open the door, experience God's comfort, and comfort others as you have been comforted.

A *silent* struggle is a *wasted* struggle.

THINK ABOUT IT

How can your physical or mental suffering be used for the good of others?

Explain your feelings about the story of the blind man and Jesus in John 9.

Write your thoughts about the following statement, "Your mental health struggles, in God's plan, have a deeper purpose than just learning how to "get through another day."

How has God comforted you and who could use your comforting?

Even though you may not relate with the extremes of Preston and Connor's story, what is your shareable story of comfort?

CHAPTER 8: WHAT'S MY NEXT STEP?

> "The Lord directs the steps of the godly. He delights in every detail of their lives. Though they stumble, they will never fall, for the Lord holds them by the hand." (Psalm 37:13-14, NLT)

I have wrestled with how to conclude this writing, so let's return to the beginning of this book where I asked you to make two declarations.

Declaration #1: If I am mentally unhealthy, I will not be ashamed to seek help from God, professionals, and those who love me. I will not give up the fight with my thoughts.

Declaration #2: If I know someone who is struggling with mental health, I will be quick to listen and offer help. I will not remain silent, exclude, or judge.

My prayer for you is that these declarations would be more than words on a page but action steps for you to pursue. I do not pretend to understand the deepest parts of your mind, but I have prayerfully and carefully written principles that should apply in many distinct situations. Hopefully, you have already been taking steps to becoming mentally healthy and will continue to do so no matter how long it lingers. If those steps mean that you need to deepen your circle of counsel and accountability, please do it. If you know someone who is struggling, don't assume they will just get better on their own. Comfort others as God has comforted you. You may not have the words to speak, but you have the ears to hear. Sometimes listening holds as much value as speaking.

If you were to ask me what my greatest fear about a person finishing this book would be, it is that they would do ***nothing***. It is the same fear I have about myself when I know *what to do* and *how to do it* but remain unchanged. The biggest enemy to being mentally healthy may not be a lack of information but a lack of motivation. James, the brother of Jesus, wrote about a similar concern for those who read and listen to the truth.

James had been writing about the familiar pattern of temptation and trials. He uncovers a few important qualities needed while experiencing difficulty.

> "…let every person be quick to hear, slow to speak, slow to anger; for the anger of man does not produce the righteousness of God. Therefore put away all filthiness and rampant wickedness and receive with meekness the implanted word, which is able to save your souls." (James 1:19-21, ESV)

Those who are undergoing hardship should be quick to listen to the truth and slow to react with their own words. A person's tendency is to immediately verbalize their deepest emotions during trial and temptation. James advises those who follow Jesus to have ears to hear what God is saying. Some may even ignore the words of God because they blame Him for their adversity, but anger against God will not produce good behavior. Instead, a person of faith should lay aside all sin and receive the truth of God's Word, which can provide comfort and cleansing.

James details two responses to hearing the truth.

> "But be doers of the word, and not hearers only, deceiving yourselves. For if anyone is a hearer of the word and not a doer, he is like a man who looks intently at his natural face in a mirror. For he looks at himself and goes away and at once forgets what he was like. But the one who looks into the perfect law, the law of liberty, and perseveres, being no hearer who forgets but a doer who acts, he will be blessed in his doing." (James 1:22-25, ESV)

First, there is a person who only *hears* the truth. This person reads and listens to the truth of God's ways but chooses not to act (James 1:23-24). James compares the Bible to a mirror and declares that it will reflect a person's true self. Scripture exposes what is right, what is wrong, how to correct wrong behavior, and how to keep doing what is right (2 Timothy 3:16-17). A person who ignores what they know to be true is unwise.

The second response is a person who *hears* the truth and *takes action*. James calls this person a doer. Obedience to truth is foundational to faith. Without spending time in God's Word, a person will not know the truth or fulfill the purposes of God.

When James uses the illustration of a mirror, my mind always goes back to an embarrassing issue I had in high school. When I was a teenager, I struggled heavily with acne. There were not just a few spots, but my entire face was riddled with noticeable red blemishes. Every single morning, I looked into the mirror and was reminded about how much I hated myself. I despised the way I looked. I'll never forget the day I was serving in the children's area of our church and a little kid innocently said, "Do you have chickenpox?" It mortified me (I may have also made him go sit in the corner!). Unfortunately, Google did not exist, so I had to find a solution the old-fashioned way – talking to people and reading books or magazines. For more than a year, I put into practice various pieces of advice. Most of them did not work. This led to more frustration and an even stronger self-hatred. I will spare you all the details, but after staying motivated to find a solution, the problem began to clear up. Eventually the red blotches were completely gone, but I have permanent scarring because of the time that passed before a solution and the severity of the problem. I've often wished that those scars would go away, except they are a reminder.

Scars remind us that we are not where we would like to be, but we are not where we once were. We should be okay with that.

I could say the same about my mental health (and maybe yours). I may not be where I want to be, but I am not where I once was. Being able to say this begins with action instead of apathy. We cannot achieve progress without first committing to change and moving toward what we know to be best. Andy Stanley puts it this way, "To get from where we don't want to be to where we do want to be requires two things: time and a change of direction." [xi]

In this book, I have spent my time helping you develop attitudes to being mentally healthy. Now it is time to take action and put into practice what you have been learning. This will not happen without the power of the Holy Spirit producing these attitudes in you as you give Him control.

What is your next step? Please allow me to conclude with *four action steps that will help you find your way to being mentally healthy*.
1) Practice Spiritual Disciplines
2) Surround Yourself With People You Trust
3) Get Pastoral and Professional Counsel
4) Embrace Messy Faith

PRACTICE SPIRITUAL DISCIPLINES

Amid your struggles with mental health, do not abandon the basic disciplines of the faith. Although you may not always feel like developing your spiritual habits, consistency and time will help you remain on stable ground. What are the spiritual disciplines that will help you grow in faith? Dr. Don Whitney, author of *Spiritual Disciplines for the Christian Life* and *Praying the Bible*, answers that very question.

> "The spiritual disciplines are those practices found in Scripture that promote spiritual growth among believers in the gospel of Jesus Christ. They are habits of devotion, habits of experiential Christianity that have been practiced by God's people since biblical times."[xii]

The most influential and transformational spiritual disciplines, in my opinion, are as follows.
1) Reading the Bible (God Speaking To You)
2) Praying (You Speaking To God)
3) Memorizing Scripture (God Shaping the Way You Think)
4) Obeying God (You Changing the Way You Act)

I do not intend to make this a dissertation about spiritual disciplines because I have written extensively and even developed a resource for these disciplines called *The Bible Reading and Prayer Journal: 40 Days of Following Jesus*. No matter what, you need to have a plan that will discipline you to think and act like Jesus. Spiritual disciplines replace unhealthy thought patterns with truth. I am not saying that reading your Bible and praying will take away your struggles, but what you gain through them is a new perspective of coping with them.

Here are a few other suggested resources to help you establish spiritual disciplines.

Download the YouVersion app and find a Bible reading plan to begin. They have hundreds of plans to fit any schedule or time of life.

Download or purchase one of my other books to keep you connected with God. I have written several books that take you chapter by chapter through a book of the Bible. It has been my passion to help people interact with God daily and these books give you a plan. You can visit tomhogsed.co to find all the current titles available or visit my author page on Amazon at amazon.com/author/tomhogsed.

SURROUND YOURSELF WITH PEOPLE YOU TRUST
Everyone needs someone in their life that they can trust. You may or may not already know this individual. If you do, be thankful and eager to share some mental health disorders you are battling. A trusted friend will accept you for who you are and walk beside you when times are tough. This could be a spouse, best friend, mentor, parent, or another connection.

What if you do not have anyone? My advice is to find yourself a supportive church. I have been a pastor for over two decades and there are plenty of people inside churches willing to come alongside those who are trying to become mentally healthy. If you are not religious, maybe join a mental health support group in your area. You should not only find a competent leader, but people who have been where you are.

GET PASTORAL AND PROFESSIONAL COUNSEL

If you are concerned about the stigma with seeing a counselor, you do not have to tell anyone you are going. I believe that some stigmas in our society regarding counseling have changed, but I realize that some people are very private about their mental health.

Being part of a church family should allow you to connect with someone who is a pastor, whether the lead or assistant. After listening to a person's needs, I always try to give them immediate steps to take; however, I also recommend professional counseling in some cases. If you seek professional counsel, try to see someone who leans into faith and advises you from the Scriptures.

The other thing to remember about counseling is that it is not an overnight but over time commitment. Do not go one time and expect to be mentally healthy the next morning. A good rule to live by is that if you commit to go once, commit to go a second time. My recommendation, depending on the severity of the problem, would be to commit to at least 6-12 months of counsel for a mental health disorder. This will give you time to create better thought patterns, establish trusted relationships with others, and develop consistent spiritual habits.

Here is something you can do right now. Pick up the phone and call your church and a counselor. You can do this later, but there is no moment like this moment.

EMBRACE MESSY FAITH

Kristen grew up in Texas. Everyone went to church there, at least that's the way it seemed to a ten-year-old girl in 1984. Kristen and her friends did not know what it was like to go without. As far back as she could remember, Kristen had everything she needed and even things she wanted. Her parents had been married for 21 years and she rarely remembered them fighting. When they argued, it never lasted more than a few minutes. Kristen's two older brothers were close to graduating from the local Christian school with honors. She never recalled either of her siblings getting into much trouble, except the one time her oldest brother arrived home an hour after curfew. Her dad was mad about that for a day, but he got over it.

Kristen loved her life, although she spent most of it isolated from the "real world." She wouldn't describe her life as problem-free, but everything always worked out. Church, Christian school, and home were the places that consumed most of her time. TV, music, and movies were closely monitored to make sure she didn't see or listen to anything that she should not. Kristen owned a few cassettes that she sticker-labeled Amy Grant and Michael W. Smith, but the music recorded on them was Van Halen on one side and Huey Lewis and the News on the other. Life was good for Kristen, at least the life she thought she knew.

Right before Kristen turned eighteen, her mom suddenly announced that she was filing for divorce and moving out in a few weeks. Kristen did not know what to think. She thought their life was complete and wondered where her parents had gone wrong. On the surface there were no warning signs, but problems are not always visible. Kristen was the only child left in the home since her brothers were away at college, so it left her to process this on her own.

Kristen's story could probably be repeated hundreds of times over. There are thousands of people who will be surprised today by some devastating news they receive – divorce, death, loss of a job, a cheating spouse, unexpected medical bill, betrayed trust, or a hundred other scenarios. These unwanted happenings can change the trajectory of a person's life, moving them from *peace* to *worry* and from *stability* to *uncertainty*. These transitional seasons can move an individual to face thinking patterns that are scary and leave them feeling alone.

Life is messy.

While some people struggle with being mentally healthy based on circumstances, others experience a mind on edge with no clear explanation. It's mostly a slow fade until a person wakes up one day and realizes that they are not where they once were. The good memories of the past are there, but no evident purpose for the future is known, leading many to question their purposefulness in this new season of life. Depression, anxiety, and despondent thoughts become commonplace. It's not like they chose to feel this way, but somewhere along the journey their outlook changed.

Life is messy.

Giftwrapping has never been that important to me, but I have been the recipient of packages wrapped with amazing attention to detail. I am the type of gift-giver who would give an item to someone in the bag I bought it in, but my wife says that is inappropriate. I believe that most of us look at life like a perfectly wrapped gift with a bow on top. It's just perfect…until it's not. Have you ever observed the aftermath of Christmas morning? Wrapping paper is scattered all over the floor. Bows have been untied. Boxes have been demolished. The gifts inside those boxes are still there, but now a little harder to see through the mess.

The good gifts God has given us – love, grace, mercy, forgiveness, second chances, hope, peace, and much more - are still there, but it is easy for them to get lost in the messiness. Jesus never promised that life would be easy; however, this life is not as good as it gets for those who are God's children. Those who have a relationship with God through

His Son, Jesus, have an eternal home where the cares and concerns of this life will be put to death.

> "And I heard a loud voice from the throne saying, 'Behold, the dwelling place of God is with man. He will dwell with them, and they will be his people, and God himself will be with them as their God. He will wipe away every tear from their eyes, and death shall be no more, neither shall there be mourning, nor crying, nor pain anymore, for the former things have passed away.'" (Revelation 21:3-4, ESV)

Is your mind on edge? In this moment, it may seem like there will never be an end to the thoughts that run through your head and the feelings that overwhelm you. Throughout this book, I hope you have seen that circumstances and feelings cannot always be changed, but our attitude toward them can. Rather than spending all your time trying to change outcomes, let God change your heart through the power of the Spirit that lives inside you.

> "Dear brothers and sisters, when troubles of any kind come your way, consider it an opportunity for great joy. For you know that when your faith is tested, your endurance has a chance to grow. So let it grow, for when your endurance is fully developed, you will be perfect and complete, needing nothing. If you need wisdom, ask our generous God, and he will give it to you. He will not rebuke you for asking." (James 1:2-5, NLT)

Your mental health battles are an opportunity to develop joy, endurance, maturity, dependence, and wisdom.

Do not give up.

Do not lose heart.

Do not believe that it will always be this way.

If your thoughts are out of control, step back from the edge and invite God to change your attitude, even when your circumstances do not change.

THINK ABOUT IT

In your own words, write out the declaration you will make based on what you have discovered while reading this book.

Since all of us may have a tendency to hear the truth but not do anything about it, what action steps will you take right now to keep up the fight to being mentally healthy?

What are your plans to make spiritual disciplines a part of your daily life?

Who is the person you trust the most to help you in your pursuit of being mentally healthy?

Will you set up an appointment with a spiritual advisor and a professional counselor? Why or why not?

RESOURCES FOR MENTAL HEALTH

"Where there is no guidance, a people falls, but in an abundance of counselors there is safety" (Proverbs 11:14, ESV).

These resources are provided as a service and support to the reader, but I am not responsible for the reliability, content, or outcome of the provided resources.

ONLINE RESOURCES

American Academy of Child and Adolescent Psychiatry
aacap.org

American Foundation for Suicide Prevention
afsp.org

American Association of Christian Counselors
aacc.net

FINDING Balance (Help for Eating Disorders)
findingbalance.com

Know the Signs (Suicide Prevention Support)
suicideispreventable.org

Mental Health America
mentalhealthamerica.net

Real Warriors - Veteran Support
realwarriors.net

PHONE NUMBERS

2-1-1 (Provides free and confidential information and referral for mental health services, help with food, housing, employment, counseling, and more)

Child-Help USA (Crisis line assists both child and adult survivors of abuse, including sexual abuse; also provides treatment referrals)
1-800-422-4453

National Alliance of Mental Illness
1-800-950-6264

National Counsel on Alcohol & Drug Dependency
1-800-622-2255

National Domestic Violence Hotline
1-800-799-7233

National Suicide Prevention Lifeline
1-800-273-8255

Self-Harm Hotline
1-800-366-8288

Veterans Crisis Line
1-800-723-8255 (Press Option 1)

Crisis Text Line 24/7 (text with a trained crisis counselor)
Text HOME to 741741
Veterans Crisis Line 838255

LEAVE ME A REVIEW

If you have enjoyed reading this book, consider writing a brief review on Amazon or another outlet. Your reviews assist others who may be looking for books and resources to help them find their way back to being mentally healthy. Thanks for taking time to read and review!

ABOUT THE AUTHOR

Although Tom grew up in Charlotte, North Carolina, he currently resides in Northeast Ohio. He holds a B.A. in Youth Ministry and M.A. in Biblical Exposition. He has been married to his wife for over 20 years and they have two children. His ministry journey began when he served as a high school pastor in Ohio for nearly 14 years. In 2008, Tom and a team of 30 people planted The Summit Church (North Canton, Ohio), where he now serves as Lead Pastor. He also founded 3-A-DAY, which helps people better understand the Bible by providing resources that take approximately 3 minutes a day to read.

Tom enjoys a variety of hobbies, including listening to all types of music, writing, messing with electronics, and watching British TV. Some highlights of his life have been his mission travels outside of the United States to places like Mexico, Argentina, Bahamas, Peru, Dominican Republic, Italy, and Ireland. Many of these trips have made a great impact on his life.

Website: tomhogsed.co
Facebook: facebook.com/tomhogsed
Amazon Author Page: amazon.com/author/tomhogsed
Twitter: @tomhogsed

MORE BOOKS BY TOM HOGSED

Be sure to check out the other books written by Tom. You can get them on Amazon or visit tomhogsed.co for the latest releases.

31 Days To Reconnect With God

Do you feel distant from God...like you need to reconnect with Him? This devotional book includes 31 daily writings to help you reconnect with God and refocus your mind on His ways. Each daily reading has six short steps to help you get back on track - receiving peace from God, reading a portion of the Bible, reviewing the truth of Scripture, responding in prayer, remembering a thought for the day, and recording your own thoughts. This book is a great start for those who may need to take a month of self-evaluation and establish the habit of reading/applying God's Word once again.

Bible Reading and Prayer Journal: 40 Days of Following Jesus

Are you looking for a way to develop and organize your spiritual disciplines? This journal will help you better organize the time you spend with God and bring 4 Spiritual Disciplines (Reading the Bible, Praying, Memorizing Scripture, Obeying God) into one place so you can focus on spending time with God rather than trying to discover how to do it. The Bible Reading and Prayer Journal also includes extensive direction and resources to the reader: How To Spend Time With God, How To Use the Journal, Sample Journal Entry, 40 Days of Journaling Pages, Bible Reading Resource List, Bible Reading Plans, Suggested Verses to Memorize, A Guide to Prayer, and Prayer Request Journal.

Spiritual disciplines don't become habits overnight. You must stay consistent and quickly pick yourself up if you get off track. It will be hard. It will take determination. It will take commitment. But, you CAN do it.

A Story of Beginnings: The Book of Genesis
Be immersed in the first book of the Bible, which sets the foundation for the rest of God's Word. As you travel back in history, your journey will lead you to places that cause you to understand God's love for mankind and His passion to redeem those who are far from Him.

Our Journey Home: The Book of Revelation
Join us on a unique journey to discover future prophetic events God revealed to the Apostle John in a series of visions almost 2,000 years ago. The book of Revelation pulls the curtain back and allows the reader to see what happens at the end of the world and where people will spend their eternity - with or without God.

The Way to Life: The Gospel of John
Take a journey into the life and ministry of Jesus as He puts His power on display and reveals His true identity as the Savior from sin. This book will show how a person can have a relationship with this Jesus and live with Him forever.

In the Light | In the Dark: The Book of Joshua, Judges, Ruth
Follow the ups and downs of God's people as they experience reward for living in the light of obedience and judgment for living in the darkness of disobedience. You will be challenged to live life God's way.

The Practical Christian Life: The Book of James
Discover the secret to overcoming trials and living out your faith every day. You'll move through topics such as temptation, showing favoritism, watching your mouth, the brevity of life, and so much more.

ENDNOTES

[i] "What Is Mental Health?" | *MentalHealth.gov*, https://www.mentalhealth.gov/basics/what-is-mental-health.

[ii] "Learn About Mental Health - Mental Health - CDC." *Centers for Disease Control and Prevention*, Centers for Disease Control and Prevention, www.cdc.gov/mentalhealth/learn/index.htm.

[iii] "Mental Health: Types of Mental Illness." *WebMD*, WebMD, https://www.webmd.com/mental-health/mental-health-types-illness#1.

[iv] "What Is Mental Health?" | *MentalHealth.gov*, https://www.mentalhealth.gov/basics/what-is-mental-health.

[v] *The Holy Bible: English Standard Version: The ESV Study Bible*. Wheaton, Ill.: Crossway Bibles, 2008.

[vi] Ducharme, Jamie. "5 Ways Love Is Good for Your Mental and Physical Health." Time, 14 Feb. 2018, time.com/5136409/health-benefits-love/.

[vii] MacArthur, John. *The MacArthur Study Bible: New King James Version*. [note on Romans 8:28] Nashville: Word Bibles, 1997.

[viii] Walvoord, John F., Roy B Zuck, and Dallas Theological Seminary. *The Bible Knowledge Commentary: An Exposition of the Scriptures*. New Testament ed. [note on Romans 8:31-32] Wheaton, IL: Victor Books, 1985.

[ix] Walvoord, John F., Roy B. Zuck, and Dallas Theological Seminary. *The Bible Knowledge Commentary: An Exposition of the Scriptures*. New Testament ed. Note on John 9:2-3. Wheaton, IL: Victor Books, 1985.

[x] Walvoord, John F., Roy B. Zuck, and Dallas Theological Seminary. *The Bible Knowledge Commentary: An Exposition of the Scriptures*. New Testament ed. Note on 2 Corinthians 1:3-4. Wheaton, IL: Victor Books, 1985.

[xi] Stanley, Andy. *Principle of the Path: How to Get from Where You Are to Where You Want to Be*. Thomas Nelson, 2011.

[xii] Whitney, Don. "What Are Spiritual Disciplines?" *Ask Pastor John*. December 31, 2015. https://www.desiringgod.org/interviews/what-are-spiritual-disciplines

MY NOTES

CPSIA information can be obtained
at www.ICGtesting.com
Printed in the USA
LVHW090157190919
631565LV00001B/70/P